D1278618

Electronic Finance
A New Approach to Financial Sector Development?

Stijn Claessens
Thomas Glaessner
Daniela Klingebiel

The World Bank
Washington, D.C.

Discussion Papers present results of country analysis or research that are circulated to encourage discussion and comment within the development community. The typescript of this paper therefore has not been prepared in accordance with the procedures appropriate to formal printed texts, and the World Bank accepts no responsibility for errors. Some sources cited in this paper may be informal documents that are not readily available.

The findings, interpretations, and conclusions expressed in this paper are entirely those of the author(s) and should not be attributed in any manner to the World Bank, to its affiliated organizations, or to members of its Board of Executive Directors or the countries they represent. The World Bank does not guarantee the accuracy of the data included in this publication and accepts no responsibility for any consequence of their use. The boundaries, colors, denominations, and other information shown on any map in this volume do not imply on the part of the World Bank Group any judgment on the legal status of any territory or the endorsement or acceptance of such boundaries.

ISBN: 0-8213-5104-4
ISSN: 0259-210X

Stijn Claessens is a Professor at the University of Amsterdam. Thomas Glaessner is a Lead Financial Economist at the World Bank. Daniela Klingebiel is a Senior Financial Economist at the World Bank.

Library of Congress Cataloging-in-Publication Data has been applied for.

Contents

Figures

Boxes

Foreword

Electronic financial services whether delivered online, through mobile phones or other remote mechanisms, or through smart cards have spread quickly in recent years. This e-finance revolution is dramatically changing the structure and nature of financial services around the world. The effects are not limited to industrial countries and advanced emerging markets. Already, countries with underdeveloped financial systems are using e-finance to leapfrog in some areas. In Africa electronic cash and other smart and even chip cards are being offered as savings and payment services for low-income customers who do not have access to formal bank accounts. Other experiences as in Brazil, Estonia, and the Republic of Korea suggest that e-finance can be introduced quickly even where basic financial infrastructure is weak or nonexistent. Technological advances are also making it possible to deliver financial services from offshore, providing some emerging markets with the additional benefits of international technology and oversight.

The World Bank is helping countries benefit from these new developments in a number of ways. Realizing the gains from e-finance will require changes in public policies toward financial services. Better regulation will be needed in such critical areas as the telecommunications framework, information infrastructure, payment systems, and competition policy. The Bank s advisory services are being adjusted to reflect the new possibilities and changed public policy priorities. This work involves diagnoses, under way in some countries, of infrastructure s readiness to support e-finance and related advice on needed policy changes. Much of the focus will be on actions that can improve the ability (through lower costs and increased competition) and willingness of private institutions to broaden access to financial services.

The Bank has also been helping countries deal with the implications of e-finance for the development of their capital markets. These efforts will increasingly be coordinated with the operations of the International Finance Corporation (IFC). Furthermore, the Bank s extensive experience in using and applying technology in its funding and investment operations is being leveraged in our advisory work. More generally, the Bank s efforts in this promising area will involve cross-departmental and multidisciplinary approaches to address this new phenomenon in the needed comprehensive way.

As part of this effort, and to advance the dialogue on the issues raised by e-finance, Bank Group staff have prepared a number of papers, one of which is presented here. This paper, and others on this topic, do not represent the World Bank Group s policies. Rather, they have been developed to stimulate discussion and solicit the views of the development community on the opportunities offered by e-finance for better financial sector development, sustained growth, and reduced poverty.

Although many questions remain to be answered, this paper contributes to the literature by laying out the policy issues in e-finance. It will be of particular interest to policymakers involved with financial regulation, but should also be of concern for those more generally interested in the potential and implications of this phenomemon.

Cesare Calari
Vice President, Financial Sector
The World Bank

Abstract

In recent years electronic finance especially online banking and brokerage services has reshaped the financial landscape around the world. This paper reviews these developments and analyzes their implications for consumers, governments, and financial service providers. First it reviews the e-finance (r)evolution in emerging and other markets and projects its future growth. Then it analyzes e-finance s impact on the structure of and competition in the financial services industry. After that it assesses how e-finance, and globalization more generally, affects financial sector policies in emerging markets including the need for changes in the approach to financial sector development. The paper then examines government s changing role in the financial sector and identifies opportunities that e-finance offers countries to leapfrog. Finally, the paper includes for policymakers and others involved in financial sector reform in emerging markets detailed information and Web links on public policy activities related to e-finance.

Acknowledgments

This paper has drawn on a wide variety of sources. The authors are grateful to the numerous authorities and individuals in many industrial countries and emerging markets who have been so kind to share their time with us and provide useful data and background material. The authors are also grateful for the many valuable written and other inputs from Fatouma Toure Ibrahima, Zeynep Kantur, Tom Kellermann, Juliane Kraska, Ying Lin, and Olga Sulla. Helpful comments and contributions were provided by Hanny Assaad, Gerard Caprio, Rodrigo Chaves, Loic Chiquier, Carlos Cuevas, Simeon Djankov, Karen Furst, Joselito Gallardo, Charlie Guarrigues, Andrew Hughes Hallet, Patrick Honahan, Leora Klapper, Jeppe Ladekarl, Bruno Lanvin, Ignacio Mas, Donald McIsaac, Daniel Nolle, Mehmet Ozkaya, Andrew Procter, Larry Promisel, Roy Ramos, Bertrand Renaud, Antony Santomero, Sergio Schmukler, Andrew Sheng, Peer Stein, Panos Varangis, and John Williamson. The authors would like to thank Paul Holtz of Communications Development Incorporated for editorial assistance and Talfourd Pierce and Rose Vo for crucial aid in preparing the manuscript for publication.

Executive Summary

Electronic finance is spreading quickly...

Electronic financial services, whether delivered online or through other remote mechanisms, have spread quickly in recent years. Despite differences across countries including such factors as the readiness of telecommunications infrastructure and the quality of regulations there is much commonality and convergence in the spread of e-finance.

E-finance penetration varies by type of service. Most affected have been brokerage markets, where online trading is becoming the norm. Increased connectivity has also accelerated the migration of securities trading and capital raising by emerging markets to a few global financial centers, with capital raised offshore by emerging markets increasing dramatically since the early 1990s. This shift has resulted in far greater integration and intermarket links. Consolidation is also occurring in key middle and back office functions such as custody, clearing of trades and retail payments, and central securities depositories.

The spread of online banking services has been more varied across countries. Spurred by the entry of new providers from outside the financial sector, however, many financial service providers are now offering e-finance services.

...and shows enormous potential

By 2005 online banking could account for 50 percent of the market in industrial countries, up from 9 percent today, and for 10 percent in emerging markets, up from 1 percent. With better connectivity, online banking in emerging markets could rise even further, to 20 percent by 2005. Similarly, in industrial countries the share of online brokerage could rise from 28 to 80 percent, and in emerging markets from 2 to 15 percent. With a better business and enabling environment, the share of online brokerage in emerging markets could even hit 40 percent by 2005.

But these averages hide big differences, depending on whether a country s penetration rate has already passed a critical level. In Nordic countries, for example, online banking could reach nearly 80 percent by 2005, while U.K. and U.S. penetration would approach just 50 percent. For online brokerage, penetration rates in Nordic countries could hit 90 percent.

E-finance is dramatically changing the structure and nature of financial services

- E-finance will lead to much lower costs and greater competition in financial services through both new entry from outside today s financial sector and greater competition among incumbent financial service providers. These developments will force banks to lower fees and commissions because providing e-finance is much cheaper than providing traditional financial services. As a result incumbent financial institutions will likely experience a sharp decline in revenue.

- Internet and related technologies are more than just new delivery channels they are a completely different way of providing financial services. Using data mining techniques, for example, providers can tailor products without much human input and at very low cost. They can also better stratify their customer base and allow consumers to build preference profiles online enabling far more personalized pricing of financial services and much more effective identification of credit risks. The Internet also allows new financial service providers to compete more effectively for customers. All these forces are delivering large benefits to consumers of financial services at the retail and commercial levels.

- Technological advances are also changing the face of the financial services industry. New providers are emerging within and across countries, including online banks, online brokerages, and companies that allow consumers to compare financial services such as mortgage loans and insurance policies. Nonfinancial entities are also entering the market, including telecommunications and utility companies that offer payment and other services. Vertically integrated financial service companies are growing rapidly and creating synergies by combining brand names, distribution networks, and financial service production.

- Trading systems for equities, fixed income, and foreign exchange are consolidating and going global. Trading is moving toward electronic platforms not tied to any location. Electronic trading and communication networks have lowered the costs of trading and allow for better price determination.

- The Internet and other technological advances have shrunk economies of scale in the production of financial services. Lower scale economies have increased competition, particularly among financial services that can easily be unbundled and commoditized through automation including bill payment services, mortgage loans, insurance, and even trade technology. Competition is further fostered by declining up-front costs. In contrast, network externalities exhibited by financial services such as payment services, trading systems, and exchanges tend to hamper competition.

Underdeveloped financial systems can exploit opportunities for leapfrogging

The effects of e-finance are not limited to industrial countries and advanced emerging markets. For countries with underdeveloped financial systems, e-finance offers opportunities to leapfrog. Such systems tend to do a bad job of allocating resources and have high intermediation costs, problems with establishing credible supervision, and possibly large fiscal costs from bank recapitalizations. For such countries, e-finance can be a revolution and evidence indicates that this is starting to happen. In Africa electronic cash and other smart cards offer savings and payment services to low-income customers including in remote areas who often do not even have formal bank accounts. Other countries Brazil, Estonia, Republic of Korea suggest that e-finance can be introduced quickly even where basic financial infrastructure is weak. E-finance will also allow financial services to be delivered to such countries from offshore, providing the additional benefits of international technology and oversight.

But realizing the gains will require changing public policies toward financial services...

The most pressing policy issues involve the enabling regulatory environment for e-finance. Adjustments are needed in approaches to telecommunications, security and related infrastructure for electronic transactions, information and privacy, and contract enforcement.

In addition, steps should be taken to minimize risks for consumers and investors, adjust prudential regulation, and improve the performance of markets.

- The telecommunications framework should avoid protecting incumbent providers and allow private firms to enhance connectivity using forms ranging from fixed lines to mobile and satellite.
- Internet transactions require security measures in cases where innovative approaches to public and private partnerships will be necessary. For example, government actions are needed to set up a framework for digital signatures. In addition, there will be a need to establish secure systems for certification, and a number of solutions involving the private and public sectors will be possible. Finally, there will be a need to address the challenges of enforcing standards for electronic security and creating a database to benchmark electronic security systems.
- If information is good enough, e-finance will extend the reach of financial institutions and capital markets. Governments will need to review their information and privacy policies in light of the new possibilities.
- With e-finance, contract enforcement has become more important within and across borders, but new technology may also help solve contract enforcement problems. Most rules will have to be set at the global level.
- Managing risks will become more important to protect consumers and investors. E-finance can increase long-standing risks such as theft and lack of privacy as well as create new ones. Thus more emphasis is needed on better disclosure, education, and information. The Internet is starting to provide solutions, with firms acting as certification agents, aggregators, and vendors of security and privacy hardware and software on behalf of consumers, investors, and financial service providers.
- Prudential regulation will probably become less effective, so it will be important especially in emerging markets to ensure that the financial sector safety net is not extended to nonfinancial firms that increasingly provide near substitutes for financial services, including deposits.
- To make financial markets and institutions work better, more emphasis should be placed

on competition policy and clear rules for markets.

...and adjusting government's role in the financial sector

Government intervention in the financial sector has generally had poor results. Government ownership of banks retards financial sector development and increases the risk of financial crises. Efforts to reach underserved groups often fail or are captured by special interests, and can incur large fiscal costs.

■ E-finance reduces the need for government intervention because the private sector can provide financial services even when a country s financial sector is weak. Market failures will be less likely because new technology will make information more easily available and, with related reforms, of higher quality. This will permit financial services to be provided more widely and make markets to trade risks and assets more complete, reducing the need for government intervention.

■ But there will still be scope for government action beyond setting the enabling environment. As a start, government could improve the way it shares information (such as credit-related information, subject to privacy statutes). And existing infrastructure, such as post office networks, can provide access to e-finance services.

■ Government s role can change fundamentally with less need for direct provision in areas such as banking services, housing finance, insurance, nonbank financial services (factoring, leasing), storage finance, trade finance, small and medium-size enterprise lending, and even microlending. In all these areas more efficient delivery of services can achieve savings, cut costs, and expand access.

With the potential of e-finance, however, come some provisos. First, e-finance offers many opportunities but it is no panacea. Most of the benefits, such as widening access to financial services, can be realized only if complementary reforms are made in communications infrastructure, security, contract enforcement, corporate governance, and other areas. Second, this paper covers a variety of issues, each of which requires further research and analysis (often multidisciplinary). Finally, as with any new phenomenon, e-finance faces large data problems so the data presented here must be viewed with caution. More efforts are needed to develop a consistent methodology for measuring concepts such as Internet penetration and related basic data on e-finance.

The Recent Past and Possible Future of Electronic Finance

This section addresses several questions: To what extent have technological advances in financial services spread, and what is the current penetration of e-finance in industrial countries and emerging markets? What are connectivity rates across countries, and to what extent has capital migrated offshore? What is the growth potential for e-finance? And what effects will e-finance have on the world s financial services industry particularly on the revenues of today s financial institutions?

E-finance has spread quickly in a diverse range of countries

Although there has been some retrenchment in the technology sector, technology continues to transform the production and delivery of financial services. Electronic financial services, whether delivered online or through other remote mechanisms, have spread quickly in recent years. As with any new phenomenon, data on e-finance are hard to collect and even harder to compare across countries and services. (For example, no standards have been developed for the measurement of such concepts as Internet penetration and related e-finance services.) Thus data should be interpreted with caution.

Using various sources, Table 1 shows the extent of electronic banking and brokerage services in key industrial countries and emerging markets. There is significant variation, with differences not clearly related to each country s level of development. In some countries, industrial as well as developing, electronic delivery of financial services remains in its infancy. Meanwhile, other countries have seen rapid penetration of e-finance. In Sweden e-finance accounts for more than one-third of financial transactions. In some emerging markets, such as the Czech Republic, Republic of Korea, and Mexico, e-finance penetration is also high for some financial services.

There is evidence of convergence in e-finance across countries. Despite institutional disadvantages (such as weaker telecommunications infrastructure) and more adverse demand and supply factors, Internet-based services are sometimes as popular in emerging markets as in industrial countries or even more popular. For example, online banking is nearly as widespread in Brazil as in the United States. Such findings suggest that around the globe, e-finance is fairly easy to introduce and for customers to assimilate. Moreover, in countries with weak financial services, customers may have a strong incentive to move to e-finance providers. Banking services may still be limited in these countries, but e-finance offers an opportunity to expand access.

Although online-only banking has been less successful than was anticipated, with several online-only banks running into difficulties, incumbent banks are starting to offer financial services electronically. The threat of new entrants has led many banks to offer e-finance ranging from basic to fully integrated Internet services. Speed and other factors influencing this shift vary with an institution s size and circumstances, but this trend has accelerated recently in Europe and the United States (Furst, Lang, and Nolle 2000; Salomon Smith Barney 1999). Thus customers of incumbent banks in other markets could soon migrate to e-finance as well.

E-finance has made the greatest inroads in securities markets especially on the retail side, where online trading has quickly taken large market shares. About 28 percent of brokerage services are now provided online in industrial countries, and shares are also high in some emerging markets. The rapid acceptance of e-finance in securities markets partly reflects the technology-driven nature of these markets and the ease with which consumers can switch brokers. Moreover, the low costs of introducing standalone and integrated brokerage services have permitted rapid growth around the world. The rapid spread also suggests that the technology of e-brokerage is easy to introduce and market to users, and that cost reductions are quickly being passed on to consumers.

Other e-finance products, such as e-money, have seen various penetration rates. In some countries (Denmark, the Netherlands, Norway) e-money penetration, as measured by the number of terminal units at which payments can be made by cards, is quite high (see Table 1). In these countries e-cards have complemented or replaced existing financial services. A stumbling block to greater penetration has been standards and to some extent security arrangements. Countries with more use tend to be smaller, suggesting that it has been easier to introduce standards for e-money. But in larger countries a lack of standards and critical mass has often not allowed stored value cards to catch on. As standards are being set and security arrangements

Table 1

E-finance has achieved significant penetration in most industrial countries and many emerging markets

Income group/economy	Online banking (customers as percentage of bank customers)	Online brokerage (transactions as percentage of brokerage transactions)	E-money (number of merchant terminals per 100,000 people)	Business environment ranking, 2000–04
Industrial country average	8	27	427	8.2
Australia	4	22	10	8.1
Belgium	4	20		8.2
Denmark	6	38	1,192	8.4
Finland	20		110	8.2
France	2	18	1	8.2
Germany	12	32	73	8.3
Italy	1	16	7	7.7
Japan		32		7.4
Netherlands	15	40	1,898	8.8
Norway	8	25	1,059	8.0
Portugal	2	7	589	7.6
Singapore	5	10	332	8.6
Spain	2	8	251	8.0
Sweden	31	55	418	8.3
United Kingdom	6	26	3	8.8
United States	6	56	35	8.7
Emerging market average	5	30	71	7.0
Argentina	3			7.2
Brazil	5	6	1	6.4
China		3		5.9
Czech Republic	1	90		7.0
Hong Kong, China	5	1	351	8.5
Hungary	6		1	7.1
India	11	2		6.0
Korea, Rep. of	13	65		7.3
Mexico	3	41	2	6.8
Poland	1			7.2
Thailand	1		1	7.3
Average for all economies	7	28	333	7.7

Source: Data on online banking and online brokerage are from various sources, but mainly from DataMonitor and central banks. Data on e-money are from the Committee on Payment and Settlement Systems, Survey of Electronic Money Developments, 2000. Business environment rankings are from the Economist Intelligence Unit Country Forecast, with a score of 10 as best and 5 as poor. The rankings combine more than 70 indicators including the strength of the economy, outlook for political stability, regulatory climate, taxation policy, and openness to trade and investment to measure the expected attractiveness of the general business environment through 2004. See Annex 1 for further details.

enhanced, e-cards and other forms of e-payments are putting pressure on banks income from payment services around the world.

Connectivity is also on the rise

Around the world, consumers and countries are increasingly getting connected. Advanced countries like the United States lead in terms of the percentage of the population that owns a personal computer and has Internet access (Table 2). The density of Internet services is also highest in the most advanced countries. Among these countries, Nordic countries stand out with high connectivity. This high connectivity is augmented by the popularity of mobile phones, which are used by almost two-thirds of the people in Finland and Norway and three-fifths in Sweden. Connectivity generally declines with income, though there are exceptions. For example, Portugal has low computer ownership and Korea has high connectivity, including through mobile phones yet the two countries per capita incomes are quite similar (in 1999 Portugal s was $11,384 and Korea s was $9,878).

In many countries connectivity has been increasing sharply in recent years. Between 1995 and 1998 the percentage of people owning a personal computer in some industrial economies rose almost 60 percent. In a sample of developing economies ownership jumped 150 percent, albeit from a lower base.[1] Increased connectivity is not limited to advanced emerging markets it is also becoming important in some of the world s least developed countries. Africa Online, for example, is a growing Internet provider in Africa (outside South Africa). Access to telecommunications is being aided by new technology, such as mobile phones with increasingly large bandwidths (Box 1).

These new technologies not only allow countries to leapfrog in connectivity, they also open new channels for delivering e-finance services. In addition to Nordic countries, countries such as Cambodia, India, Malaysia, and Poland are seeing financial service providers use mobile phones to deliver financial services. Around the world,

connectivity is being further enhanced by rapid improvements in telecommunications regulation. Still, many emerging markets require substantial reforms in such regulation to enhance the enabling environment and allow the private sector to deliver financial services.

Capital raising and securities trading are migrating abroad

Technology has also driven the large migration of capital raising and securities trading to international financial centers. The share of capital raised abroad and traded offshore has been rising sharply, especially in emerging markets. Equity capital raised internationally (through American depository receipts) jumped from less than $5 billion in 1990 to nearly $30 billion in 2000 (Figure 1a). This trend has been accompanied by an even sharper increase in offshore trading, with offshore trading in

---

Box 1

Mobile phones: The developing world's technological springboard

In 1990 there were just 11 million mobile phone subscribers worldwide. By 1998 that number had jumped to 320 million, and current estimates are of more than 500 million users. Privately built wireless networks drive this growth. Mobile phones have made telecommunications available even to the world's poor, partly because of the widespread creation of telecenters and public call offices.

Recognizing the benefits, governments are adopting policies to encourage mobile telecommunications in rural areas. Policies include license obligations to serve rural communities (Mexico, the Philippines), subsidies through rural telecom development funds (Chile, Peru), variations of build-operate-transfer arrangements (Thailand), and low-interest loans. The spread of rural telecommunications is further facilitated by falling costs for mobile phones.

Some developing countries typify the possibilities of leapfrogging using mobile phones. Zimbabwe saw wireless subscribers skyrocket to 174,000 in 1999—annual growth of more than 800 percent, the fastest in the world. In Botswana, Côte d'Ivoire, and Rwanda wireless phone subscribers outnumber fixed-line users. Brazil has more than 15 million mobile phone subscribers, more than all Nordic nations combined. With a devastated fixed network after more than 20 years of civil war, adopting cellular technology was the obvious choice for Cambodia, and within a year mobile phones outnumbered fixed phones. Even though its per capita income is among the world's lowest, Cambodia now surpasses 31 countries in telephone penetration—including countries with much higher incomes.

Source: See bibliographical note.

---

1   The industrial economies were Australia, Denmark, Hong Kong (China), Japan, the United Kingdom, and the United States. The developing economies were Brazil, Chile, China, Guatemala, Hungary, India, Kenya, Mexico, Peru, Senegal, Sudan, Vietnam, and Zimbabwe.

Table 2

Consumers and countries around the world are getting better connected, 1999

Income group/economy	Personal computer use (percentage of population owning personal computers)	Internet connectivity (Internet hosts per 10,000 people)	Mobile phone use (percentage of people who are mobile or cellular subscribers)
Industrial country average	**33**	**337**	**42**
Australia	47	417	34
Belgium	32	162	31
Denmark	41	72	49
Finland	36	1,057	65
France	22	83	36
Germany	30	161	29
Italy	19	59	53
Japan	29	133	45
Netherlands	36	357	44
Norway	45	715	62
Portugal	9	50	47
Singapore	44	208	42
Spain	12	67	3
Sweden	45	488	58
United Kingdom	31	241	46
United States	52	1,123	31
Emerging market average	**7**	**31**	**16**
Argentina	5	18	12
Brazil	4	13	9
China	1	0	3
Czech Republic	11	72	19
Egypt	1	0	1
Hong Kong, China	29	120	63
Hungary	7	83	16
India	0	0	0
Korea, Rep. of	18	40	50
Mexico	4	12	8
Poland	6	28	10
Russian Federation	4	10	1
South Africa	6	34	12
Thailand	2	3	4
Turkey	3	5	13
Average for all economies	**20**	**194**	**30**

Source: International Telecommunication Union, World Telecommunication Indicators Database 1999. See Annex 1 for details.

American depository receipts reaching more than $1 trillion in 2000 (Figure 1b). In 2000 the top six emerging markets in terms of capital raised Argentina, Brazil, China, India, Korea, and Mexico collected more than $10 billion in offshore capital, and offshore trading in American depository receipts from these countries totaled $180 billion. By 2000 about 19 percent of trading in emerging market securities was occurring offshore (Table 3).

Figure 1a

Capital raised by companies in American depository receipts, 1980–2000

Billions of U.S. dollars

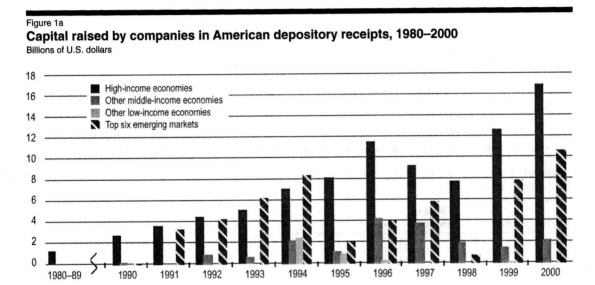

Figure 1b

Value traded by companies in American depository receipts, 1980–2000

Trillions of U.S. dollars

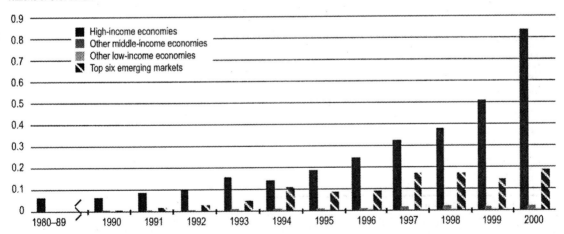

Note: Figure 1a shows the amount of capital raised in international financial markets through American depository receipts. Figure 1b shows trading on the New York Stock Exchange in American depository receipts. Data for 1980—89 are the annual average for the period. In both figures the top six emerging markets based on total capital raised in American depository receipts in 1980—2000 are Argentina, Brazil, China, India, Republic of Korea, and Mexico. The high-income economies are Australia, Austria, Belgium, Denmark, Finland, France, Germany, Greece, Hong Kong (China), Ireland, Israel, Italy, Japan, Luxembourg, Netherlands, New Zealand, Norway, Portugal, Singapore, Slovenia, Spain, Sweden, Switzerland, Taiwan (China), and the United Kingdom. The other middle-income economies are Bahrain, Chile, Colombia, Croatia, Czech Republic, Dominican Republic, Egypt, Estonia, Hungary, Jordan, Kazakhstan, Latvia, Lebanon, Lithuania, Malta, Morocco, Papua New Guinea, Peru, Philippines, Poland, Romania, Russian Federation, Slovak Republic, South Africa, Sri Lanka, Thailand, Tunisia, Turkey, Uruguay, and Venezuela, RB. The other low-income economies are Ghana, Indonesia, Malawi, and Pakistan.

Source: Claessens, Klingebiel, and Schmukler forthcoming.

This migration has generally led to gains for both issuers and investors. Issuers have seen higher prices and increased liquidity for their securities. And with remote access to global trading systems, institutional and individual investors can now execute their trades on the platforms with the best prices and execution.

E-finance has enormous potential— especially in a supportive environment

The rapid growth of e-finance reflects the expansion patterns of certain products and services with network externalities, such as telecommunications and some financial services (Furst, Lang, and Nolle 2000). Penetration for these products and services tends to accelerate once a market has reached critical mass. This critical mass and subsequent growth is often similar across markets. Most analysts expect e-finance to exhibit this same pattern of market penetration (see ongoing analysis by Forester Research, Jupiter Research, and DataMonitor).

So what determines when a country reaches a critical mass of penetration? A variety of factors, including the quality of a country s telecommunications infrastructure, its approach to regulation, and the demand for and supply of e-finance services (Sachs 2000). It is too early to

Table 3

Emerging markets' capital is increasingly owned, traded, and listed abroad, 2000

Percent

Region/economy	Share of foreign ownership	Share of foreign value traded	Share listed in New York or London
Latin America	24	54	53
Argentina	10	65	65
Brazil	28	43	63
Chile	13	55	46
Colombia	5	8	13
Mexico	42	58	48
Peru	9	59	24
Venezuela, RB	62	73	44
Asia	7	7	18
China	4	14	46
India	11	14	29
Indonesia	12	10	16
Korea, Rep. of	17	5	24
Philippines	11	14	17
Taiwan (China)	6	2	22
Thailand	12	0	0
Europe, Middle East, and Africa	15	60	50
Hungary	32	5	54
Israel	29	90	78
Poland	14	2	13
Russian Federation	14	13	88
South Africa	14	24	55
Turkey	10	1	13
All emerging markets	13	19	38

Source: Goldman Sachs Research estimates.

fully explain the determinants of e-finance penetration. Nevertheless, in countries where e-finance penetration has reached a level that should lead to faster growth, the level of connectivity and the quality of the business environment appear to explain the point of takeoff. This assessment is based on simple regression analysis using connectivity and the business environment as the explanatory variables and takeoff for online banking as the dependent variable (see Annex 1). The higher is the level of connectivity, the earlier a country reaches the point at which online banking can be expected to take off.

This relationship indicates when countries can expect a sharp increase in online banking (Table 4). For example, France can expect rapid growth by 2003, and Portugal by 2004. Russia, by contrast, will not reach the takeoff point for online banking until 2006. A similar relationship holds for the penetration of online trading, except e-brokerage appears to depend not just on connectivity but also on the business environment.

Using the actual and projected takeoff years for 19 industrial countries with extensive e-finance penetration, it is possible to project e-finance penetration for a group of emerging markets (using the typical pattern of diffusion after takeoff). These projections indicate that by 2005 an average of 50 percent of banking services will be provided online in the industrial countries and 10 percent in the emerging markets up from 9 percent and 1 percent in 2000. The change will be even more dramatic for online brokerage: from an average of 28 percent to 80 percent in the industrial countries and from 2 percent to 15 percent in the emerging markets.[2]

But these averages hide big differences between countries, depending on whether they have reached critical mass. In Nordic countries online banking will shoot from an average of 20 percent in 2000 to nearly 80 percent in 2005 (Figure 2). And in Sweden online trading will jump from 55 percent to 94 percent. But in Italy penetration in banking will rise from just 1 percent to 22 percent, because the country has not yet achieved critical mass in

e-finance. But by 2010 it might, and e-banking penetration in Italy could exceed 70 percent.

E-finance penetration could grow even faster if the environment for it improves. Figure 2 also shows the results of a simulation in which connectivity in emerging markets rises to about the level of today s lowest-ranked industrial country a rating of 6. With better connectivity the penetration of online banking in most emerging markets could rise to about 20 percent by 2005, and online brokerage could increase to about 40 percent. With a more conducive environment, e-finance penetration around the world could thus more than quadruple for banking, from 7 percent in 1999 to 30 percent in 2005, and almost double for brokerage, from 28 percent to 45 percent.

Financial institutions should anticipate lower revenues

Using new technology, new entrants will provide financial services at lower cost. Incumbent financial institutions will see pressures on their profits unless they can quickly move their business online and cut operating costs to levels similar to those of the new entrants. Leaders among incumbents in adopting new technology will challenge other incumbents through cheaper, better services. Lower revenues for incumbents could pose problems in countries where financial institutions have been sheltered from competition and where branch networks have high fixed costs.

The risks to revenues and profits will depend on the speed of penetration, the cost advantages of providing e-finance, and the ability of incumbents to adjust. The marginal costs of e-finance are much lower than those of traditional delivery channels, with each transaction costing a few cents compared with $1 or so for transactions at bank branches and $0.50 at automated teller machines. Although there are significant up-front costs, in the medium term the costs of delivering bank services online will be much lower at least as low as in today s most Internet-advanced banks, such as some in Sweden. As a result margins for banking services could fall to 1.6 percentage points (the average margin in 1997-98 in Nordic countries) or less.[3]

---

2   The 2000 data on online banking and online brokerage for emerging markets differ from those in Table 1 because Table 4 refers to a larger sample of emerging markets.

3   Margins differ by financial product; to average margins, total net internet income is calculated as a share of bank assets and then expressed in percentage points.

Table 4

The takeoff point for online banking depends on the level of connectivity

Income group/economy	Current connectivity rating	Actual or projected takeoff year	Connectivity rating with connectivity improvement	Actual or projected takeoff year
Industrial countries				
Australia	8	2001		2001
Austria	8	2001		2001
Belgium-Luxembourg	8	2003		2003
Denmark	8	1998		1998
Finland	9	1998		1998
France	8	2003		2003
Germany	8	2001		2001
Ireland	8	2000		2000
Italy	8	2004		2004
Japan	8	2001		2001
Netherlands	8	2002		2002
Norway	9	1998		1998
Portugal	6	2004		2004
Singapore	8	2001		2001
Spain	7	2002		2002
Sweden	9	1998		1998
Switzerland	8	1999		1999
United Kingdom	8	2001		2001
United States	9	2001		2001
Emerging markets				
Argentina	6	2004	6	2004
Brazil	5	2006	6	2004
China	3	2010	6	2004
Czech Republic	5	2006	6	2004
Egypt	3	2010	6	2004
Hong Kong, China	8	2001	8	2001
Hungary	5	2006	6	2004
India	3	2010	6	2004
Korea, Rep. of	7	2003	7	2003
Mexico	5	2006	6	2004
Poland	5	2006	6	2004
Russian Federation	5	2006	6	2004
South Africa	5	2006	6	2004
Thailand	5	2006	6	2004
Turkey	5	2006	6	2004

Note: Connectivity ratings are from the Economist Intelligence Unit and range from 0—10. Connectivity ratings combine ratings on computer ownership, Internet hosts, mobile phone use, and other telecommunications connectivity criteria. For industrial countries the projected takeoff year is based on the typical pattern of penetration and the country s current level of penetration (see Table 1). For emerging markets the projected takeoff year is based on the country s current connectivity rating, with the projections based on a regression analysis using the industrial countries projected takeoff year, where the regression line is estimated as $2,014.6 — 1.71 * Connectivity$ See Annex 1 for details on information sources and methodology.

Source: Authors calculations.

Figure 2
E-banking penetration: actual and projected rates for 2000, 2005, and 2010

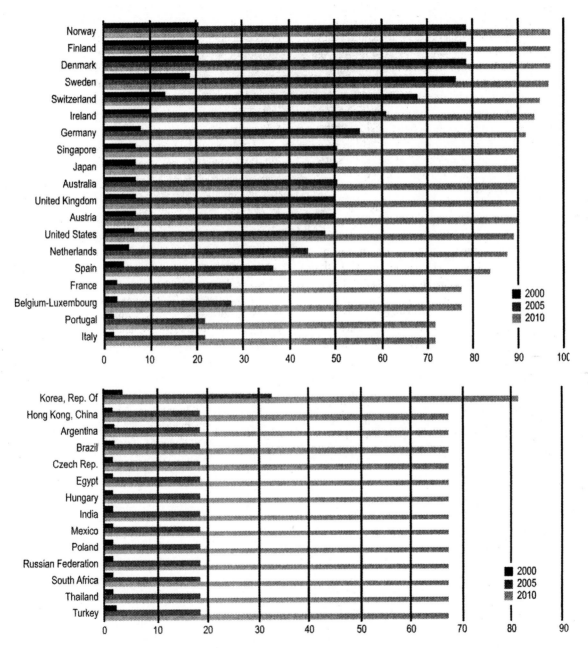

Note: The two figures show projections based on takeoff years, with connectivity in all emerging markets assumed to be at the same level as in today s lowest-rated industrial country (a connectivity rating of 6, or better if the emerging market s rating is already higher). Thus the projections lead to the same minimum level of penetration in each emerging market. This is admittedly a substantial simplification, because it assumes that all emerging markets will improve their connectivity to the same degree. It also ignores the fact that several emerging markets already have higher e-finance penetration today even though their connectivity is perhaps not as high. See Annex 1 for more details.

Source: Authors calculations.

Because today s most Internet-active banks have not completed their transformation to e-finance, their current cost structure might be higher than their long-run structure. Thus a margin of 1.6 percentage points may overestimate the marginal costs of providing e-finance services. But recent experience shows that banks may need to rely on a bricks and clicks approach that involves higher marginal costs than just the clicks part. Because Nordic counties have seen the most e-finance, their current cost structure may be most indicative of fully electronic financial service provision. Still, Nordic, Dutch, and other banks involved in e-finance are making big cuts in branches and staff (Sveriges RiksBank 2000), and further cost reductions are likely.

These margins and the above projections for online penetration rates would then imply that for banks in industrial countries, bank margins will drop from an average of 2.3 percentage points in 1997 to about 2.0 percentage points in 2005 (Table 5). Margins would fall less initially in emerging markets, from 4.4 percentage points in 1997 to 3.9 percentage points in 2005. But some countries would see more dramatic changes. In Denmark bank margins could drop by nearly half by 2005, and in Sweden and the United States margins could slide more than a quarter. By 2010 the declines would be even sharper, with especially big drops in Brazil, Denmark, Poland, Russian Federation, South Africa, Thailand, Turkey, and the United States.

For brokerage revenues, changes would be dramatic almost everywhere because penetration has been fast and costs savings large. The projections here assume that the costs of online brokerage are just 25 percent of traditional costs, which is still less than the drop in commissions in markets like the United States since online brokerage was introduced. As online brokerage proceeds, commission revenues could decline by a factor of about 2 in many countries. With higher connectivity, and expressed as a share of bank assets, brokerage revenues in industrial countries could fall from 0.1 percent to 0.05 percent by 2005 and in emerging markets from 0.19 percent to 0.13 percent.

The projected decline in revenues will not be limited to banking and brokerage. Many other financial services payments, underwriting, asset management, personal financial advice could see similar declines when they become subject to more competition from e-finance. More generally, the threat of entry has probably lowered the market value of incumbent banks and other financial service providers, suggesting that markets are expecting lower profits.

In the short run the impact on revenues will be largest in countries such as Nordic countries where e-finance has already reached critical levels. In the medium run the impact could be greatest in countries with less efficient financial services that have seen little e-finance to date. Migration and cost differences are both likely to be higher in such markets once e-finance comes onstream. In Brazil and Turkey, for example, bank margins are now more than 7.7 percentage points which helps explain the spread of e-finance and the potential for new entry by e-finance providers.

Table 5

E-finance will slash banks' net interest margins, 2005 and 2010

Net interest income as a percentage of bank assets, with connectivity improvement

Income group/economy	Net interest margin, 1997	Start of rapid growth	Net interest margin, 2005	Net interest margin, 2010
Industrial country average	**2.34**		**1.96**	**1.69**
Australia	2.03	2001	1.82	1.64
Austria	1.72	2001	1.66	1.61
Belgium-Luxembourg	1.25	2003	1.34	1.52
Denmark	4.20	1998	2.20	1.68
Finland	1.57	1998	1.59	1.60
France	3.30	2003	2.84	1.99
Germany	2.37	2001	1.95	1.67
Ireland	1.14	2000	1.42	1.57
Italy	2.74	2004	2.50	1.93
Japan	1.84	2001	1.72	1.62
Netherlands	1.62	2002	1.61	1.60
Norway	2.55	1998	1.82	1.63
Portugal	1.81	2004	1.76	1.66
Singapore	2.30	2001	1.95	1.67
Spain	3.19	2002	2.62	1.86
Sweden	2.46	1998	1.82	1.63
Switzerland	1.75	1999	1.65	1.61
United Kingdom	2.57	2001	2.09	1.70
United States	4.06	2001	2.91	1.87
Emerging market average	**4.39**		**3.85**	**2.50**
Argentina	4.20	2004	3.73	2.46
Brazil	7.76	2004	6.63	3.63
China	2.26	2004	2.14	1.82
Czech Republic	3.04	2004	2.77	2.07
Egypt	1.73	2004	1.71	1.64
Hong Kong, China	2.90	2001	2.26	1.73
Hungary	3.65	2004	3.28	2.28
India	2.89	2004	2.65	2.02
Korea, Rep. of	1.90	2003	1.80	1.66
Mexico	3.64	2004	3.26	2.27
Poland	5.50	2004	4.78	2.88
Russian Federation	4.79	2004	4.21	2.65
South Africa	4.96	2004	4.34	2.70
Thailand	5.50	2004	4.78	2.88
Turkey	11.17	2004	9.41	4.75

Note: Assumes a level of connectivity in each emerging market equal to at least the level of today s least advanced industrial country that is, a rating of 6 (or better if the emerging market s current rating is already higher).

Source: Authors calculations.

The New World of Financial Services

As noted, e-finance has spread quickly in many countries and has enormous potential. The Internet and related technologies are more than just new delivery channels they are a completely new way of providing financial services. E-finance is also dramatically changing the structure and nature of markets for financial services. This section analyzes the effects e-finance will have on the industry s structure, on trading systems, and on competition. The focus is on industrial countries, but the section also assesses the opportunities these developments offer emerging markets to leapfrog.

A new landscape is emerging for the provision of financial services

E-finance is changing the face of the financial services industry (Box 2). New types of service providers are entering the market within and across countries, including online banks, brokerages, and so-called aggregators (which allow consumers to compare financial services such as mortgage

---

Box 2

The new world of financial service providers

Financial services are now offered through a multitude of delivery channels, from traditional brick-and-mortar branches to wireless devices. Six steps can be distinguished in the production and distribution of financial services, though in practice these steps often overlap or are vertically integrated (see Figure 3).

Access devices (rather than tellers or branches) are becoming many customers' first point of contact with financial service providers. These devices include personal computers, personal digital assistants (such as Palm Pilots), televisions equipped with Internet access, cellular phones, and other communication devices. These channels are being complemented by low-cost "branches," kiosks (standalone computers connected to bank systems), and other public access devices in supermarkets, convenience stores, and common areas (airports, train stations).

Portals are becoming the critical link between access devices and financial service companies. Portals offer access to a range of financial service providers, often for free or a fixed price, but generate revenue from fees paid by providers referred through the portal. These include specialized portals developed by financial service companies as well as general portals such as the U.S.-based America Online, Lycos, Yahoo!, and Microsoft along with others in emerging markets (Paxnet and Thinkpool in Korea, Terra in Latin America). Portal companies attempt to process and personalize information to capture consumers. Portals are proliferating rapidly, even in emerging markets. Korea, for example, is home to 300 portals, many of which function as gateways for financial service providers. In addition, customers can access financial service providers through private networks, and some providers have established their own specialized portals.

Aggregators complement portals, allowing consumers to compare mortgage, insurance, or lending products offered by financial service providers. In addition, quasi-aggregators aggregate or display prices of financial products offered by

different providers or even conduct single or block reverse auctions of mortgage loans or insurance products (as with DollarDEX in Singapore). Finally, other specialized companies are undertaking functions on behalf of large banks or insurance companies and developing online techniques to mine data and offer personalized financial products to consumers.

Financial institutions serve as conglomerate providers of financial services that are global brands (Citigroup, Deutsche Bank, Warburg) and as specialized financial service companies. Partly in response to the entry of new competitors and to reap the benefits of new technology, incumbents (banks, large insurance companies) are consolidating around recognized brand names to position themselves in an environment of increased commoditization and electronic delivery. Merrill Lynch and HSBC, for example, recently announced a joint venture in private banking that combines HSBC's network with Merrill Lynch's product range. Large telecommunications companies that already have access to a large network of customers are starting to provide payment and other services. In addition, telecom companies are forming alliances to extend their global network to financial services delivered online. Examples include Deutsche Telecom, Telefonica, AT&T, and Telemex. And increasingly specialized financial service providers—so-called mono-liners in all the main financial service areas, from mortgage loans to personal loans to insurance to brokerage to payment services—are establishing online operations.

Financial products are being commoditized or tailored to the needs of customers. Such products are distributed through specialized financial service providers and financial conglomerates.

Electronic enablers support general as well as specialized financial service providers and virtual banks. Specialized software engineering companies such as S1, Checkfree, Sanchez, and System Access provide e-finance system solutions that are completely integrated and permit the rapid adaptation needed in today's world.

Source: Claessens, Glaessner, Klingebiel, 2000.

loans and insurance policies). Nonfinancial entities are also entering the market, including telecommunications and utility companies that offer payment and other services through their distribution networks and customer relationships. To reap the benefits of the new technology, and in response to this new entry, banks, insurance companies, and the like are starting to deliver financial services electronically setting up in-house online activities or completely new ventures such as virtual banks.

Thus financial services are moving away from brick-and-mortar delivery channels to a multitude of electronic and other channels, with portals and aggregators offering new distribution and advertisement channels for financial services. Vertically integrated financial service companies are growing rapidly and creating synergies by combining brand names, distribution networks, and service production (Figure 3).

For example, companies associated with portals (America Online, Yahoo!, Microsoft) and major telecommunications companies (Deutsche Telecom, Telefonica) are developing strategic relationships and ownership links with major financial service companies, banks (such as the Bank of East Asia with Yahoo!), and each other (Telefonica and Lycos). At the same time, many major financial institutions (Goldman Sachs, Chase, Merrill Lynch, Morgan Stanley) are part owners of promising Internet startups. And goods-producing companies are taking advantage of bank distribution networks (Citidollars with a variety of consumer-related companies). These developments are changing the competitive landscape for financial services and will continue to erode the franchise value of financial service providers that are inefficient or do not adopt competitive business models (see Figure 3).

Figure 3

Different service providers and delivery channels are combining to create a new world of financial services

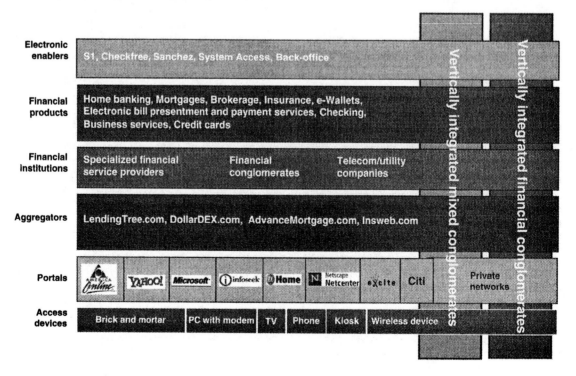

Source: Claessens, Glaessner, Klingebiel, 2000.

Trading systems are consolidating and going global—lowering costs and increasing efficiency

Driven by advances in communications technology, trading systems are consolidating and going global. Trading is moving toward electronic platforms not tied to any location. (Nasdaq s computers are based in Turnbull, Connecticut, for example, but traders are located around the globe.) New electronic systems have lowered the transaction costs of trading and allow for better price determination because electronic execution and matching techniques imply less chance of market manipulation. These advantages are more important in markets that had not yet converted to electronic trading (such as the United States) than in those where electronic trading has been the norm (such as Europe). The new technology also allows for much easier cross-border trading, and over time for intermarket trading systems.

Combined with globalization, these forces are putting pressure on incumbent stock exchanges, which have responded with mergers and alliances. Because many exchanges are self-regulating organizations, the pressures for change usually do not come from within the industry. Rather, they come from users and investors who want to pay smaller commissions, effect trades more quickly, and maintain anonymity on placed orders (Box 3).

For several reasons, competition is increasing

Smaller economies of scale

The Internet and other technological advances have shrunk economies of scale in the provision of financial services. The main financial service still exhibiting increasing returns to scale is the medium-size loan market, because large databases of credit history are required to build a credit-scoring model for medium-size clients giving lar ger lenders a potential competitive advantage. For most credit, however, economies of scale have become small because the fixed costs associated with screening small borrowers (less than $100,000) have dropped significantly.

Smaller scale economies have increased competition, particularly among financial services that can easily be unbundled and commoditized through automation. These include payment and brokerage services, mortgage loans, insurance, and even trade finance. Most of these services require limited initial capital outlays and no unique technology.

Box 3
The massive shifts in stock markets and exchanges

A revolution is under way in how financial (and nonfinancial) contracts are traded. These changes have involved traditional exchanges as well as business-to-business (B2B) transactions.

Several electronic order routing and trading networks have emerged in recent years. These networks have evolved into order-driven matching systems that are provided electronically to participants seeking anonymity. Electronic communication networks started out as pools of liquidity feeding into existing markets but now serve as alternative trading outlets in several developed and some emerging capital markets. In some markets these networks account for a large share of total trading (one-quarter of the dollar volume of Nasdaq in the United States).

Other alternative trading systems are being set up around the world, often with links to existing trading systems. For example, Instinet began as an electronic local interdealer broker and dealer but now has automatic routings to a number of stock exchanges. There is speculation that a few trading systems will soon allow investors to trade 24 hours a day. Exchanges are recognizing that their services—trading systems—are increasingly becoming a commoditized product offered through other means. Eventually, traditional stock markets such as the New York Stock Exchange will cease to exist in their current form.

Reflecting these competitive pressures, and the more general desire for increased liquidity through larger markets, many stock exchanges in industrial countries have established links, merged, or even demutualized (that is, become for-profit organizations rather than cooperative, not-for-profit organizations). Recent examples include the mergers between the Amsterdam, Brussels, and Paris exchanges (resulting in the creation of Euronext) and joint ventures and alliances between Nasdaq and stock exchanges in Australia, Canada, Hong Kong (China), and Japan. Similarly, the stock exchanges in Singapore and Australia recently agreed to cross-list all traded shares. And the New York Stock Exchange has formed alliances with the Tokyo Stock Exchange, Hong Kong Stock Exchange, Australia Stock Exchange, Toronto Stock Exchange, Mexico Bolsa, São Paulo (Brazil) Bovespa, and Euronext to trade through linked exchanges 24 hours a day. The consolidation of these markets—accounting for more than 60 percent of global market turnover—is leading to a smaller number of very large markets.

Source: Claessens, Glaessner, Klingebiel, 2000.

Lower transaction costs substantially increase competition for providers and cut costs for consumers. To retain market share, online brokerages have been forced to radically restructure the way they deliver services. Commissions and fees fell from an average of $53 a trade in early 1996 to $16 in mid-1998 and by mid-2000 some online brokerages had lowered their commissions to zero. Electronic communication network commissions, now $0.05 a trade, are continuing to fall. Barriers to entry based on ownership of physical facilities are disappearing, and incumbent institutions are being forced to merge or in some cases to demutualize to have a chance of remaining viable.

Shrinking up-front costs and changing entry barriers

Web-based financial services unify the Internet as a communication standard by combining a Web browser, a display standard, and a Web server as the access point to back-end operational systems. As a result cross-selling of products becomes easier and economies of scope increase.

In the past, sunk costs were important entry barriers in the financial services industry. Examples of sunk costs include branch networks, knowledge about local borrowers, access to payments systems, branding advantages involving large up-front advertising expenses, perceptions of size and safety, long-lasting customer relationships, and substantial up-front investments in technology. But sunk costs are becoming less important, partly because electronic delivery modes do not rely on branch networks (Table 6).

At the same time, new entry barriers are being created through first-mover advantages. Once a new entrant is an established service provider, other new entrants will have to spend a lot on advertising to attract new customers (as E-trade and Ameritrade

Table 6

The Internet is changing features of financial services

Service	Economies of scale	Commoditization	Up-front costs; branding, advertising	Network externalities
Retail services				
Payments	●●	●●●●	●●	●●●●
Loans and mortgages	●●	●●●●	●●	●
Discount brokerage services	●●	●●●●	●●●	●●
Investment advice	●●	●●●	●●●●	●●
Mutual funds	●●	●●●	●●●	●●
Insurance	●●	●●●	●●●	●●
Wholesale services				
Commercial lending				
• Large	●●	●●●	●●	●
• Medium-size	●●●	●●●	●●	●
Corporate services (underwriting, mergers and acquisitions advice, risk management)	●●	●●	●●●●	●
Large-value payment systems	●●●	●●●	●●●●	●●●●
Markets				
Trading systems and exchanges	●●	●●●●	●●●	●●●●
B2B exchanges	●●	●●●●	●●	●●●●
New services				
E-payment providers	●●	●●●	●●	●●●●
Electronic enablers	●●	●●	●●	●●●
Financial portals	●	●	●●●	●●●●
Aggregators	●●	●●●	●●	●●

Note: ● = none, ●● = low, ●●● = medium, and ●●●● = high.
Source: Authors assessments.

have done in the United States). Services such as underwriting and mergers and acquisitions advice exhibit low levels of commoditization and still require relationship capital, a certain size, and a brand name to compete effectively. But these services enjoy few or no network externalities and are increasingly subject to global competition. The scope for a contestable market then depends on the size of the market. A limited number of financial institutions involved in underwriting, but operating on a global basis, present a very different competitive environment than would a few players in a small market (say, less than $1 billion).

Higher network externalities

Although declining economies of scale, increasing standardization and commoditization, and falling up-front costs foster competition, this need not be the case for services that exhibit network externalities. A financial service exhibits network externalities if the value of the service rises with the number of market participants using it. Payment services, for example, have decreasing economies of scale, low up-front costs, and easy commoditization. But payment services are subject to large network externalities, because the value of electronic payment services largely depends on the degree to which users adopt a common standard. The financial service provider that manages to create this common standard will end up with a large share of the market, decreasing competition. Similar characteristics apply to trading systems and exchanges (traditional or B2B), to financial portals, and to a lesser extent to e-enablers (see Table 6).

Emerging markets have new opportunities to leapfrog

Most of the discussion above reflects current trends in advanced industrial countries; as such it does not address the possibility of leapfrogging. But several emerging markets show that e-finance penetration can proceed much faster than is implied by the preceding analysis. Brazil, Estonia, and Korea have already moved beyond levels predicted on the basis of their current connectivity and business environment (Box 4).

The diversity in these three countries levels of development, with per capita incomes ranging from $3,500—10,000, suggests that leapfrogging is possible for many other countries as well. It might even be that what appear to be disadvantages, such as poor financial services and weak financial infrastructure, actually accelerate the move to e-finance. Just as in securities markets, where rapid migration offshore has partly been a response to weak market infrastructure and poor corporate governance, many consumers could move quickly to e-finance delivered in part from remote locations. But leapfrogging will not just emerge spontaneously it may require changes in policies for financial sector development.

Box 4
Leapfrogging around the globe: Estonia, Republic of Korea, and Brazil

Estonia has made impressive progress in information technology. After communism collapsed, this nation of 1.5 million people moved straight to wireless technologies, and almost 30 percent of the population now owns a mobile phone. In addition, about 35 percent has access to Internet services. E-finance has also taken off. Five of Estonia's seven banks offer online services, making for more than 250,000 Internet banking clients—a penetration rate almost as high as in the advanced Nordic countries. As elsewhere, banks in Estonia see online banking as a cost-efficient way of expanding, avoiding expensive new branch offices.

In Korea the number of people banking online shot up from 120,000 at the end of 1999 to 4 million at the end of 2000. Over the same period the number of transactions increased

from 700,000 to 32 million a month. Online trading has been growing exponentially, with more than 65 percent of brokerage transactions now conducted online. This revolution has been facilitated by the fact that while only one in five Koreans owns a personal computer, more than half have a mobile phone.

Bradesco, Brazil's largest private bank, is the world's third largest Internet bank, with 1.7 million clients banking online. Bradesco provides its more than 700,000 corporate clients with a business to business site offering brokerage, insurance, and pension fund services used by more than 800 companies, and a business to consumer site that facilitates financial transactions for 1,000 companies. Bradesco places its transaction payment services on smart cards that consumers can download from their computers.

Source: See bibliographical note.

Changes Needed in Financial Sector Policies

The recent patterns and future potential show that e-finance could deliver large gains to consumers while changing the role of financial institutions. The potential is especially large for countries lacking well-functioning, efficient financial systems with wide access. But achieving the full gains of e-finance requires changing the model for financial sector development.

Many questions need to be addressed. Are there now better ways of building a robust, efficient financial system that provides wide access to a broader set of consumers of financial services? What public policies best facilitate such a process? Will some traditional policy areas be less important? How will areas of emphasis differ by the level of development of a country s financial sector? Which policy prescriptions are more important for countries with better services and wide access, and which are more important for countries with limited financial infrastructure and little or no well-functioning financial system? In all cases, what policy changes should be made to avoid unnecessary risks and allow for the greatest gains? And what policy changes have countries already made in response to e-finance?

Moving from an institutional to a functional approach

The traditional approach to financial sector development has been institution oriented, with a heavy emphasis on developing commercial banks (Box 5). The institutional approach is increasingly being overtaken in industrial countries by the functional approach (Merton 1995). In that approach financial services are unbundled into their various functions with their own production structures, not necessarily associated with any particular type of financial institution.

The range of institutions offering financial services has also broadened, with less emphasis on commercial banks as financial service providers relative to large financial conglomerates or increasingly specialized entities in areas such as asset management, brokerage, and insurance. This commoditization of financial products and functions is changing public policies toward financial sector development in industrial countries.

Rapid technological change and the Internet are making the functional approach relevant for emerging markets as well. First, local institutions

have become less important. Basic financial services can now be efficiently produced and delivered from remote locations over the Internet. More sophisticated services, such as securities trading and asset management, can be produced in and delivered from a few global financial centers reducing the need for local systems and associated investments in human and physical capital. Second, a financial system need no longer be built around banks, which used to be considered special. Rather, governments can focus on how financial services can be provided most efficiently, regardless of the location or the entity providing the service.

Table 7 summarizes how the new paradigm differs from current approaches to financial sector development, with the last column showing areas of emphasis of various international working groups (see also Annex 2). The changes in public policy for financial sector development will vary by the stage of development of a country s financial sector. To really benefit from e-finance, emerging markets will need a significant change in emphasis. For more developed financial systems that already have sophisticated services, wide access, much of the infrastructure to support e-finance, and much innovative e-finance already occurring, public

---

Box 5

The institutional approach to financial sector development

Most of the public policies used to foster financial sector development have been based on an institutional approach. This approach focuses on creating effective local institutions (commercial banks) that provide payment services, intermediate resources, and help overcome problems of asymmetric information. At the same time, these banks are often considered special (given their role in the payments system and credit intermediation) and are protected by a public safety net, necessitating the development of good regulation and supervision.

But creating credible, effective regulation and supervision has proven difficult in many emerging markets, as shown by many costly banking crises. The development of other institutions—brokerage firms, investment banks, leasing companies, insurance companies, pension funds, exchanges, and a host of other institutions and related legal frameworks—has been supported by changes in overall legislation and actual institution building. Examples of institution building include the establishment of private entities (investment banks, stock exchanges), public development banks, and other public intermediaries and the provision of special lending windows.

Source: Claessens, Glaessner, Klingebiel, 2000.

Table 7

A new paradigm is emerging for financial sector development

○   Not important or not addressed
●   Somewhat important
● ●   Important
● ● ●   Very important

Area	Current paradigm	New paradigm	Working groups
Creating an enabling environment			
Regulatory framework for telecommunications	○	● ● ●	●
Security framework and public key infrastructure	○	● ● ●	● ●
Framework for information and privacy	●	● ● ●	● ●
Framework for contract enforcement	●	● ● ●	●
Financial system laws that are institution specific	● ● ●	● ●	● ●
Market infrastructure	● ● ●	● ●	● ●
Risks at the consumer, investor, and institution levels			
Consumer protection	● ●	● ● ●	● ●
Investor protection	● ●	● ● ●	● ●
Prudential regulation	● ● ●	● ●	● ● ●
Markets—functioning, performance, and risks			
Competition policy	●	● ● ●	○
Functioning and volatility, rules for markets, liquidity, transparency, access, disturbances, liquidity risks, stress properties	● ●	● ● ●	●
Forms of government intervention			
Development banks, public microlending institutions, and directed credit	● ●	●	○
Information provision and "collateral" institutions	● ●	● ● ●	○
Modifying use of existing institutional infrastructure	● ●	● ● ●	○

Source: Authors assessments as the area relates to financial sector development. For working groups column, the assessments are based on various reports issued by international working groups and bodies (see also Annex 2).

policy changes will be more evolutionary and less pronounced, with many already under way. These advanced countries still need policy changes, however.

Although the emphasis will vary by each country s stage of development, key reforms will often include creating an enabling regulatory environment, minimizing risks for consumers, investors, and institutions, and improving the performance of markets especially in terms of competition policy. In addition, the role of government needs to be reconsidered.

Creating an enabling regulatory environment

The most important areas of the regulatory framework for e-finance are telecommunications,

security and related public and private key infrastructure, information and privacy, and contract enforcement. In addition, financial system laws and market infrastructure will remain important, though less so than in the past. Countries are making progress in these areas.

Telecommunications

Telecommunications regulation for both fixed and nonfixed lines is a key area for e-finance. [4]

---

4   A full treatment of these issues is beyond the scope of this paper. An excellent reference beyond documents issued by the International Telecommunication Union is Intven, Oliver, and Sepulveda (2000).

As noted, nonfixed lines are providing new opportunities in developing countries, including in remote areas in Africa, China, and many less developed Asian countries such as Cambodia. Regulation must privatize post and telegraph administrations, improve licensing of competitive operators, enhance mandatory interconnections and unbundle public switched telephone networks, implement independent regulatory bodies, and implement proper pricing regulations (Box 6). Improving access to telecommunications for a larger portion of the population is especially important in emerging markets.

Electronic security and infrastructure

Both providers and consumers of e-finance view security as a constraint and a concern. Serious operational risks and potential liabilities are associated with security breaches in the transfer of funds or instructions and the actual theft of identification information over the Internet (Furst, Glaessner, and Kellermann 2001). In response, encryption techniques and various protocols (secure socket layer, Financial Interchange Extended language) have been developed by the private

sector, but evidence on intrusions suggests that these may not be sufficient. Actual penetrations into banks are understated because of the damaging implications for banks reputations.

For the whole set of security arrangements that is, the so-called public key infrastructure to work, four functions must be present: authentication (knowing the parties when exchanging information), integrity (messages cannot be changed during transmission), nonrepudiation (agreements cannot be later denied), and confidentiality (messages cannot be read or copied by unauthorized users). Authentication has been perhaps the most difficult to address.

One approach to improving authentication that is being employed is the use of public and private keys. Authorities will have to address three main issues in designing a country s public key infrastructure. First, adequate penalties are needed for unauthorized access to or tampering with computer systems and Websites penalties akin to those for other crimes. Second, a proper certification process is needed for public and private keys, as are secure systems for storing such keys and adequate cross-certification for private key

---

Box 6

Enhancing connectivity in emerging markets by improving telecommunications regulation

Connectivity can be enhanced through a combination of telecommunications policies:

- Anticompetitive behavior by incumbent telecom companies—charging excessive rates for interconnections, refusing to build or make available adequate interconnection capacity, refusing to unbundle network elements or services needed for efficient interconnections—has retarded or prevented competition in telecom markets in many countries. Mandatory interconnections and unbundling of public switched telephone networks are needed to make the sector more competitive.
- Many emerging markets have not yet privatized telecommunications. Privatization is essential for making telecom services more efficient, because without it competition will be hindered and key services will be costly—widening the digital divide.
- In many countries the licensing of competitive operators must be enhanced to give domestic and international telecom providers sufficient incentives to compete within and across media—fixed line, cellular, and so on.

- Regulatory authorities must be independent, and regulatory processes must be transparent. To enhance the governance of such agencies—a complex issue in emerging markets—certain international and objective standards must be applied in such areas as interconnections, licensing, and pricing.
- Price cap regulations that ensure price increases for telecom services are in line with general price changes can make services more efficient and reduce regulatory lags. Such regulations should not, however, place undue discretion in the hands of telecom companies or regulatory authorities.
- Targeted universal access funds may help increase access to telecom services in countries with great income diversity. Chile and Peru provide examples of effective funds.
- Removing barriers to trade in telecommunications and harmonizing competition policy on a global basis will help. Under the auspices of the European Commission and the World Trade Organization, standards are being developed to define market dominance and identify barriers to competition.

Source: Intven, Oliver, and Sepulveda 2000.

providers. This can involve a single public certification authority but need not: several countries are successfully operating multiple private and public agencies.[5] Third, government may need to set minimum authentication or certification standards while preserving incentives for private solutions. Regulations should be flexible enough to allow for creative use of new technologies (such as biometrics) in improving authentication processes.

Information and privacy

E-finance makes it easier to manage customers and to customize products. For example, a financial institution linked with an Internet service provider can use information culled from a customer s Web use to offer the customer new financial products. But such efforts must respect people s desire for privacy and confidentiality. Information about a person or business can increasingly be seen as a property right that people can voluntarily share with others. That property right must be clearly defined through information and privacy standards.

Such standards should address four issues: notice, choice, access, and security. Individuals must be given notice of what information is being collected and how it is being used. They need to be given a choice of whether to allow such collection. Once the information has been collected, the provider of such information must have access to it, and the collector must ensure its security.

Privacy standards will mainly require private sector actions, but these need to be backed by government privacy frameworks within and across countries (Box 7). Moreover, privacy and secrecy laws should not become barriers to the development

of e-finance. Thus general secrecy laws, along with other statutes such as bank secrecy laws, need to permit the sharing of not only negative but also positive credit information. As the Internet expands, standards for information and privacy will increasingly need to be global.

Box 7

Privacy problems—the role of the public sector and private solutions

Many countries have started to adapt their privacy statutes to the Internet. Although progress is uneven and national statutes differ, an international move toward more homogeneous standards is under way. The International Labour Organization, International Telecommunication Union, Universal Postal Union, and World Trade Organization are developing in their specific areas of concern common standards for a privacy law. In addition, the Council of Europe and the United States are developing the first international treaty on cyber crime.

Still, country approaches vary. In the United States self-regulation and sector laws have generally been used to ensure adequate privacy. An exception is the Gramm-Leach-Blily Act, which requires the U.S. Securities and Exchange Commission to issue regulation that applies to broker-dealers, investment companies, and registered investment advisers (financial institutions). This regulation protects all "nonpublic personal information" about consumers, including information that consumers provide to financial institutions, results of transactions performed for consumers, and any other information about consumers that financial institutions obtain outside public channels.

By contrast, the European Union has favored much more comprehensive privacy legislation enforced by freestanding data protection agencies. The European Union's privacy directives also authorize the cutting off of data flows to countries not in compliance with EU standards. To avoid a trade war over personal data and interruptions in companies' data flows, the United States and the European Union have devised a safe harbor agreement.

The private sector has played an important role in providing solutions to privacy issues on the Internet. New technologies have created new risks for privacy, but they can also provide private solutions. In the United States many Websites certify companies or e-commerce sites as having good practices for information privacy (for example, TrustE, at www.truste.com) or provide consumers with tips on safeguarding their privacy (for example, the Electronic Frontier Association). Many new companies offer software to ensure anonymous browsing, disable cookies, and even develop personal or company firewalls to enhance e-mail security. Direct government monitoring of privacy guidelines and private solutions have different costs and benefits, and thus can complement each other.

Source: OECD 2001.

---

5   Certification authorities can be government agencies (such as postal authorities), technology providers (such as GTE or Verisign), telecom service providers (such as Nortells Entrust), or financial service providers themselves. The certification authority authenticates the public key by distributing it with a certificate that it digitally signs. The potential liability of the certification authority and the reputation implications of security breaches have been used as an argument for outsourcing the public key infrastructure to private providers. Banks that are certification authorities include ABN, Bank of America, Deutsche Bank, Barclays, Chase Citigroup, and Hypoverensbank.

Contract enforcement

Poor contract enforcement hinders finance and commerce regardless of the delivery channel. But new technology can lower the costs of contract verification and enforcement. The Internet increases the amount and speed of available information and can easily link disparate sources of information. It can assist, for example, in the automation and efficiency of registries. With digital signatures, credit risk assessments can be made much faster and more efficient. In addition, the Internet and global financial service provision allow for collateralized loans extended from remote locations. E-finance will thus make cross-border dispute resolution and contract enforcement more important. The North America Free Trade Agreement (NAFTA) and EU experiences provide useful examples of how to address these issues.

Technology can help enforce contracts directly. When foreclosing because of late payments, for example, a lender can use remote devices to shut off and track down a leased car. Technology also allows for better methods of ensuring perfection of a security interest in collateral in a dematerialized environment, because databases can be linked directly. Finally, smart cards and other multipurpose cards use technology to bypass many standard contract enforcement mechanisms, which may explain their popularity in Africa.

Financial and market infrastructure

Laws and systems are a crucial element of financial infrastructure. As noted, e-finance will allow for a more functional, rather than institutional, approach to financial sector development. This implies that the laws governing financial contracts will become more important than the laws governing institutions that operate in the financial sector. Laws on secured transactions and capital market dealings, for example, will become more important than laws on commercial banks and insurance companies.

To date the impact of new technologies has been most pronounced in wholesale and securities markets, but gains are also becoming evident in retail markets. In Estonia and Finland, for example, many retail financial transactions are done electronically. A good technology infrastructure thus becomes key. Finally, linking financial service providers or more broadly , entire financial systems in emer ging markets to countries with more sophisticated technology will allow them to benefit without having to invest in expensive systems and demanding oversight structures. Stock markets in smaller emerging markets, for example, could be linked to and integrated with those in larger markets.

Progress to date

A recent survey of 23 countries, including 15 emerging markets, shows that few have addressed all the aspects of these key areas for creating an enabling environment (Table 8). But progress is being made in many areas, and over time that will allow the full benefits of e-finance. Digital signature laws, for example, are being introduced in many countries, often based on model laws promulgated by the United Nations Commission on International Trade Law (UNCITRAL). Privacy and confidentiality laws are also being adjusted. And while all these areas are important, progress in all of them is not a precondition for e-finance. In some countries with otherwise underdeveloped financial infrastructure (lack of clearing, custody, and settlement arrangements, weak payment systems), developing communications and public key infrastructure can be sufficient to allow the import of many financial services and related forms of financial infrastructure.

Minimizing risks for consumers, investors, and institutions

E-finance can create new risks, whether at the level of a financial service of fered at the retail or wholesale level or at the level of an institution. Reducing these risks will require authorities to focus more on better disclosure, protection, and education for consumers and investors, as well as better risk management by providers of financial services. All these issues will need to be addressed at an increasingly global level.

E-finance also calls for rethinking approaches to prudential regulation and issues related to extending the financial sector safety net (Claessens, Glaessner, and Klingebiel 2000). The second point is especially important in many emerging markets given their often extensive safety nets. Balancing short-run financial stability with longer-run incentives will be challenging during this shift in the form of and approach to regulation and supervision.

Table 8

Progress is being made in creating an enabling regulatory environment

Region/country	Do electronic signatures or online verification of people exist?	Does a secrecy law exist, and has it been modified to address issues raised by e-finance?	Can financial service providers obtain positive (A) or negative (B) information on borrowers?
Europe			
Czech Republic	Pending	Yes	No
European Union	Yes	Yes, but not modified	△
Finland	Yes	Yes	Yes to both
France	Yes	△	Yes to both
Germany	Yes	△	△
Hungary	Pending	Yes	Yes to both
Poland	Pending	Yes	Pending
Russian Federation	Pending	No	△
Sweden	Yes	Yes	Yes to both
Turkey	No	Yes	Yes to B
United Kingdom	Yes	Yes	Yes to both
Americas			
Argentina	Pending	Yes	Yes to both
Brazil	Pending	Yes	Yes to B
Mexico	Yes	Yes	Yes to both
United States	Yes	Yes	Yes to both
Asia			
Australia	Yes	Yes	Yes to both
China	Pending	Yes	Yes to both
Hong Kong, China	Yes	Yes	Yes to B
India	Yes	No	Pending
Japan	Yes	Pending	Yes to both
Korea, Rep. of	Yes	Yes	Yes to both
Singapore	Yes	Yes	Pending
Africa			
Morocco	No	No	No
South Africa	Pending	No	Yes to both

△ Not enough information was available to determine the answer.

Source: World Bank survey. More detailed descriptions of respondents replies are available from the authors.

Consumer protection

E-finance and related innovations have made it possible to stratify customers through electronic customer relationship management and to customize financial services. These developments can create risks for consumers. For example, information from an online bank account could be misused in others parts of a financial institution or elsewhere.

At the same time, technological developments make it easier for authorities to enforce existing regulations protecting customers because electronic audit trails are assured and Internet service providers can be required to provide information to authorities. Furthermore, many companies are offering smart agents that enable consumers to search for and compare alternative products offered on the Internet cutting search costs and empowering consumers.

Policy decisions must reflect the choices of consumers and the incentives of financial service providers and Internet service or application software providers. The key policy step will be to require increased disclosure and greater transparency on the terms of financial services offered over the Internet. Better privacy and security standards will also help consumers.

Rules are also needed that limit the scope for conflicts of interest within financial institutions and between financial institutions and Internet-related firms. For example, limits may be needed on cross-selling products within financial institutions. Governments may also need to clarify the liability of financial service providers for services contracted out, such as Internet banking software, as recommended by the Electronic Banking Group of the Basel Committee on Banking Supervision.

E-finance can more easily involve outright fraud, theft, and other abuses hurting small consumers and impinging on the confidence in and use of e-finance. Actions such as the development of a cyber-force (as is becoming common among securities regulators) can help weed out the worst offenders and send clear signals. But there will remain severe limits on government s ability to prevent misuse, making disclosure more necessary (see Annex 2 for international working group efforts in this area). These risks also highlight the need for more extensive consumer education, which could be provided through creative private-public partnerships.

Investor protection

As with consumer protection, issues relating to investor protection and education will take on much greater importance because new risks are particularly difficult to monitor in emerging markets. In a more global and electronic world, regulatory and supervisory approaches and philosophies will have to put much greater emphasis on disclosure, the quality of information, the timing and release of material information, the definitions and obligations of investment advisers and managers, and governance and conflicts. Much greater emphasis will also need to be placed on

reducing legal and regulatory impediments to cooperation in cross-border securities enforcement and to harmonizing legal and regulatory treatment of Internet-related securities transactions across borders.

E-finance has also led to a range of questions on how to oversee the many new infomediaries directly or indirectly involved in providing financial services. Links between portals, Internet service providers (ISPs), telecommunications and software providers, financial service companies, and specialized online brokers are becoming more ubiquitous but they raise new risks. Many portals and Internet service providers, for example, have exclusive links with financial service providers. Will those links create conflicts?

Other questions arise. Should a portal or Internet service provider be allowed to charge for leading customers to an electronic brokerage in what amounts to online order routing? And if so, under what forms of securities regulations? When a portal undertakes offline business that involves underwriting debt or shares, its incentives may be skewed toward its online services. How can electronic initial public offerings (IPOs) and road shows be properly regulated and supervised? Similar complications, not all new, arise when advertising borders on investment advice. And when is the use of an electronic bulletin board by an issuer only providing a forum and when is it a platform soliciting investors for an electronic offering? Can a portal refuse to allow advertising by certain financial service providers? Box 8 outlines some of the guiding principles developed to date, some of which have been laid out by the International Organization of Securities Commissions (see Annex 2) and other regulatory authorities.

Prudential regulation and the safety net

Of particular short-run importance in prudential regulation are changes needed to prevent the new risks posed by e-finance. Much of the work on such risks is occurring in international forums such as the Electronic Banking Group of the Basel Committee on Banking Supervision (Box 9). Important risks identified by the group are operational risks related to the increased use of technology (including the greater reliance on outside vendors), legal and reputation risks, and conflicts that may be introduced by the electronic delivery of financial

Box 8

Securities regulation, the Internet, and emerging markets

Some basic principles have been developed to guide securities regulators in markets that have experienced rapid growth in connectivity and widespread electronic distribution of securities-related financial services (see Annex 2 for Internet principles established by the International Organization of Securities Commissions). In protecting investors, it is useful to distinguish between the responsibilities of three groups: broker-dealers that provide online brokerage services, Internet service providers or portals that provide online order routing services to brokers or are themselves involved in offline services, and issuers (or underwriters) that distribute their securities publicly or privately over the Internet.

Online brokers' communications with investors should satisfy the principles of notice (timely and adequate notice that information is available electronically), access (access given electronically should be comparable to that available in other forms), and evidence to show delivery (reason to believe that delivery requirements will be satisfied). When financial information is delivered electronically, there must be adequate protections for privacy and confidentiality. In many countries self-regulating organizations (often exchanges) have been encouraged to work with issuers and related brokerage firms and investment banks to establish review committees that determine whether market participants meet requirements for proper communication and advertising to investors. In many cases written policies have been required of broker-dealers as well as a pre-use review process and even "fair disclosure" guidelines to ensure that all material nonpublic information is disclosed simultaneously across all forms of communications. In some countries even public disclosure reports on broker-dealers must be posted on Websites to allow for better-informed investors. "Suitability" and "know thy customer" rules are also important. These rules often oblige brokers to make certain determinations—such as ascertaining investors' financial status, tax status, investment objectives, and any other information deemed reasonable—before making a transaction recommendation. In many

countries questions arise on how this process can be made more efficient—through use of other authentication processes, including digital signatures—and not require physical interaction with investors.

Online order routing by an associated Internet service provider or portal in exchange for a fee raises the question of whether this constitutes provision of brokerage services. Many countries are starting to view such arrangements as brokerage unless the portal does not recommend specific securities or participate in any financial services offered by the ultimate provider. Complicating matters, the extensive offline businesses of many portal companies can create conflicts about the accuracy of the company information they report. This problem makes regulatory oversight difficult—and is becoming more common in emerging markets that have seen a rapid increase in financial service portals. Korea, for example, is home to 300 such portals.

Online securities offerings can lead to conflicts of interest. Many securities issuers advertise using electronic bulletin boards, but this can be viewed as an offering. In general, issuers that use electronic bulletin boards on the Internet are being asked to maintain some status with regulators. They also need to provide on their Websites financial information required of registered issuers, keep records of quotes, provide no advice on buying or selling securities, receive no compensation for creating the bulletin board, and receive and transfer no securities on behalf of third parties. Third-party bulletin boards are complex to regulate because they may be acting as an exchange, alternative trading system, or broker-dealer. In addition, online offerings of securities through an initial public offering (IPO) or a private placement or offering raise regulatory and supervisory challenges. Similarly, attention must be paid to stock purchase plans, stock giveaways, electronic road shows, and offshore or cross-border offerings over the Internet. Much of this will require developing global standards, taking into account issues such as differences in the definition and treatment of solicitations.

Source: U.S. Securities and Exchange Commission 2000; IOSCO 1998.

services. Most of these risks are not new, but e-finance intensifies them.

For the future, regulations relating to disclosure and timing of information and to governance and conflicts will become more important, altering the traditional approach to bank supervision and regulation. This shift will be accompanied by risks of reduced profitability for existing financial institutions a trend under way for a long time. But e-finance could sharply accelerate the drop in profits, so the Electronic Banking Group has identified strategic and business risks as one of the main risks of e-finance.

Some aspects of prudential regulation are becoming more important, while others may need to be reviewed in a new light, particularly in emerging markets. This is especially true for the financial sector safety net, defined here to include policies on deposit insurance, lender of last resort facilities, and government s role in the payments system at the wholesale level and the exact conditions under which it will guarantee payments.

In the past the need for a financial sector safety net and associated prudential regulation and supervision has arisen from the need to treat deposit-taking institutions differently from other

Box 9

Principles for managing risk in online banking

A recent report by the Electronic Banking Group of the Basel Committee on Banking Supervision identifies 14 key risk management principles for online banking. Banks and their supervisors should consider these principles when formulating risk management policies and processes for online activities.

■ **Management oversight.** Effective management oversight of the risks associated with e-banking needs to be in place, and e-banking risk management should be integrated with overall risk management.

■ **Management of outsourcing and third party dependencies.** Comprehensive, well-defined, ongoing oversight is needed for managing outsourced relationships and third party dependencies supporting e-banking, including adequate prior due diligence.

■ **Segregation of duties.** Appropriate measures are needed to ensure proper segregation of duties in e-banking systems, databases, and applications.

■ **Proper authorization measures and controls in systems, databases, and applications.** Appropriate authorization measures and proper controls need to be in place for e-banking systems, databases, and applications.

■ **Clear audit trail for e-banking transactions.** A clear audit trail is needed for all e-banking transactions.

■ **Authentication of all entities, counterparts, and data.** Banks should authenticate the identity and origin of all entities, counterparts, and data transmitted over the Internet.

■ **Nonrepudiation (accountability) for e-banking transactions.** Nonrepudiation should be ensured to hold users accountable for e-banking transactions and information.

■ **Comprehensive security control.** Banks should ensure the appropriate use of activities and properly safeguard the security of e-banking assets and information.

■ **Integrity of transactions, records, and information.** Banks should prevent unauthorized changes to and ensure the reliability, accuracy, and completeness of e-banking transactions, records, and information.

■ **Appropriate disclosure.** To avoid legal and reputation risks, including for cross-border activities, banks should have adequate disclosure for e-banking services.

■ **Confidentiality and privacy of customer information.** The confidentiality of customer information and adherence to customer privacy requirements should be ensured.

■ **Business continuity and contingency plans to ensure the availability of systems and services.** Plans should ensure that e-banking systems and services are available to customers, internal users, and outsourced service providers when needed.

■ **Incident response planning.** Incident response plans should be in place to manage and minimize problems arising from unexpected events—including internal and external attacks that hamper the provision of e-banking systems and services.

■ **Role of supervisors.** Bank supervisors should assess banks' management structures, practices, internal controls, and contingency plans for e-banking.

Source: Electronic Banking Group of the Basel Committee on Banking Supervision; see also Annex 2.

economic agents and from banks special role in the payments system. But banks are no longer the only institutions providing deposit-like services, and many substitutes for bank deposits have emerged. On the payments side, banks have become less special because mutual funds and most brokerage houses offer payment services and technological progress is enabling the further development of alternative payment mechanisms. For example, new nonbank providers of payment services use new technology (e-mail transfers, stored value cards, smart cards) to provide payment functions. Balances on stored value cards can typically be transferred without directly involving a depository institution (Osterberg and Thomson 1998).

These developments raise the question of which payment services should fall under regulatory oversight and what institutions should have access to the payments system. Decisions about which alternative services to regulate will matter a lot,

particularly if the regulation is prudential as opposed to consumer protection-related, because prudential regulation implies that the services are covered by the safety net. Since the new types of payment services cover a continuum of modalities, authorities need to carefully evaluate where to draw the line and be cognizant of a possible shifting of the line over time due to political and other pressures. Authorities should be especially wary of extending deposit guarantees to new deposit substitutes because the moral hazard implications can be substantial.

Similarly, authorities have to decide whether to open access to the payments system to nonbanks and, if so, in what form. In most countries only banks have access to the payments system, and alternative providers of payment services have to clear through banks. Restricting access to the payments system to banks allows incumbent banks to preserve a core part of their franchise value.

Allowing direct entry by nonbanks and nonfinancial companies (telecom and utility companies, brokers) will reduce the franchise value of banks and risk increasing overlap and blurring lines between financial and nonfinancial companies. This could enlarge the safety net, even if by default.

Redesigning the safety net is all the more urgent because of the risks that it will otherwise be extended in the short run rather than being reduced. Financial services have become more complex, with increasingly blurred distinctions between products and institutions and between the financial and nonfinancial companies providing these services. As financial service providers expand their activities, the safety net could be extended to nonbanking activities of financial service providers unless policies are changed. Governments may end up taking on a much larger range of risks most of them unrelated to any economic reasons for a public safety net in the first place.

Progress to date

For the most part a laissez-faire approach to regulation and supervision has been adopted for e-finance. Among countries with sophisticated financial systems, most regulatory and supervisory adjustments to address e-finance have been piecemeal (Table 9). These countries already have good financial services, and most income groups have access to at least basic financial services. As a result e-finance penetration is progressing fairly smoothly, with no big new risks having arisen. In some countries disclosure laws are being adjusted, stored value cards are being regulated, and rules for online banking are being introduced. In some cases rules are being harmonized with international standards, helping to define international best practices. But as Table 8 shows, even industrial countries have not necessarily addressed all the issues.

Industrial countries have also taken a piecemeal approach to regulating e-finance providers which means that new risks can arise. For example, some countries have not issued special legislation and related operational criteria for online banks. Many have yet to review the rules applying to infomediaries such as portals that play a direct or indirect role in providing financial services. Many countries do not have adequate laws and regulations to address possible conflicts that arise through Internet-based offerings of securities-

related services, varying from use of electronic bulletin boards to online order routing by portals to an electronic road show in the context of an electronic debt offering. Moreover, few countries have clarified whether issuers of various forms of quasi deposits or multipurpose cards will be guaranteed.

For countries with underdeveloped financial systems, e-finance offers the opportunity to evaluate the development of a safety net and the associated prudential framework more carefully. In such countries many financial services can come from nonbanks, which should not fall under a public safety net. Furthermore, in such countries financial services, and associated supervision and prudential regulation frameworks, can be imported if foreign multinational financial service conglomerates can enter or deliver services remotely a trend that has been increasing worldwide (Goldberg, Dages, and Kinney 1999).

The reduced emphasis on prudential regulation and the limits on the financial sector safety net will save not only scarce human resources but also fiscal resources. Many governments have found it difficult to credibly signal that they will not bail out financial institutions. But with less emphasis on banks and a bigger role for foreign providers of financial services, governments may find it easier to resist bailouts, save valuable fiscal resources, and improve the allocation of resources. Of course, mechanisms are still needed to ensure that financial services are imported only from good systems and to limit risks arising from links between financial institutions and nonfinancial companies.

Finally, some countries have implemented regulations that could stymie the development of e-finance. Some industrial countries, for example, have limited the establishment of online banks to existing banks, suppressing the innovation and competition that come with new financial service providers. Access to the large value transfer system can be another barrier to entry for online service providers. In the European Union money can be issued electronically only by traditional credit institutions and a new type of credit institution known as an electronic limited money institution (ELMI). But ELMIs face tougher prudential restrictions on their investments, which may hamper the spread of e-finance as it increases the cost of entry for new financial service providers.

Table 9

E-finance regulation has yet to address some outstanding issues

Region/country	Are there disclosure requirements for portals?	Is there regulation for stored value cards or electronic payments (such as deposit substitutes)?	Are issuers of deposit substitutes required to inform their customers that the cards are not guaranteed if the issuer fails?
Europe			
Czech Republic	No	Pending new Banking Act	Pending
European Union	No	Yes	No
Finland	No	Yes	Pending
France	No	Yes	△
Germany	No	Yes	No
Hungary	No	Yes	Yes
Poland	No	Pending	No
Russian Federation	No	Yes	△
Sweden	Yes	Yes	No
Turkey	No	No	△
United Kingdom	No	No	No
Americas			
Argentina	Yes	No	△
Brazil	Pending	No	△
Mexico	No	No	No
United States	Yes	No	Yes
Asia			
Australia	No	Yes	△
China	Yes	Yes	Yes
Hong Kong, China	Yes	Yes	No
India	No	Yes	△
Japan	No	Yes	△
Korea, Rep. of	No	No	No
Singapore	Yes	Yes	No
Africa			
Morocco	No	No	No
South Africa	No	Yes	Yes

△ Not enough information was available to determine the answer.

Table continues on next page

Improving the performance of markets

Although it has gotten easier to create and access markets as shown by the migration abroad of trading and listing by corporations from emerging markets they do not necessarily function properly . In emerging markets poorly defined and enforced competition policies often combine with weak corporate governance and highly concentrated ownership and wealth. Yet effective competition policies and good corporate governance are essential to achieve the gains from e-finance that come with increased efficiency, competition, and credibility. Emerging markets also harbor significant risks of local markets becoming far less

Table 9—*continued*

E-finance regulation has yet to address some outstanding issues

Region/economy	Are there separate authorization requirements for virtual providers of e-finance?	Do statutes, regulations, or guidelines address issues of outsourcing for financial institutions?	Institutions with access to the government-sponsored (and/or government-operated) large value transfer system
Europe			
Czech Republic	No	No	Domestic banks and stock exchange institutions
European Union	Same as for "brick and mortar" providers	Yes	Credit institutions and electronic limited money institutions
Finland	No (refers to EU)	△	Central Bank
France	No (refers to EU)	△	△
Germany	No (refers to EU)	Pending	Credit institutions
Hungary	No	△	Financial institutions
Poland	No	Yes	Banks and clearinghouses
Russian Federation	No	△	Bank of Russia clients
Sweden	No (refers to EU)	△	Credit institutions
Turkey	No	No	Banks
United Kingdom	No (refers to EU)	△	Banks
Americas			
Argentina	No	△	Banks and clearinghouses
Brazil	No	Yes	△
Mexico	No	No	Banks and brokers
United States	Pending	Yes	Depository institutions
Asia			
Australia	No	Yes	Depository institutions
China	No	No	Banks
Hong Kong, China	No	Yes	Depository institutions
India	No	△	Banks
Japan	Yes	Yes	Financial institutions
Korea, Rep. of	Pending	Yes	Commercial banks
Singapore	Yes	Yes	Banks
Africa			
Morocco	No	No	Banks
South Africa	No	△	Banks

△ Not enough information was available to determine the answer.

Source: World Bank survey. More detailed descriptions of respondents replies are available from the authors.

liquid and more subject to insider dealing. Moreover, e-finance and increased connectivity can raise risks of market fragmentation and volatility. And across borders, there is a need to harmonize market standards and practices. How can these weaknesses be addressed?

Competition policy

As noted, recent changes are making financial services more like other goods and services and financial markets more like nonfinancial markets. Technology is leading to specialization in the provision of financial services and to the development of separate markets, particularly wholesale markets, insulated from other financial markets.

These developments make competition policy for financial services more feasible. At the same time, the speed and associated benefits of technological innovation in financial service provision are increasingly becoming a function of the degree to which entry by new entities financial and nonfinancial is allowed. This is making competition policy more important but, as noted, also raises issues for the extension of the financial sector safety net.

Competition tests require defining a product and its market. But it is getting harder to precisely define financial products and their markets. Many traditionally nonfinancial services are taking on characteristics of financial contracts. The creation of cash equivalents, derivative markets in weather and power (such as enermetrix.com), and other derivative contracts settled in cash defy classification into distinct categories of financial or nonfinancial services. The continuum from cash (notes) to stored value cards to barter-type arrangements competing not just as cash substitutes, but also along many other dimensions, makes it hard to precisely define the concept of payment services or even deposits.

It is obviously difficult to define entry barriers for services that cannot be well defined. Moreover, market sizes are changing. Changes in delivery modes for retail financial services are lowering entry barriers for many financial services that were once local, making traditional measures of market concentration meaningless. As noted, many markets have gone global, making it more difficult to geographically define markets. In countries such as New Zealand and in some Latin American and Eastern European countries, foreign banks account for more than two-thirds of local markets.

With markets going global, nontariff and nonquantity barriers have become more important for financial services. The ability of foreign financial institutions to provide financial services on a global basis can be hampered by differences in laws (such as in bank secrecy laws and in know thy customer provisions related to money laundering and fraud), regulations, and conventions. Globalization raises the importance of such structural barriers because they can hinder competition. But such differences are not easy to measure or likely to be harmonized in the short run.

Empirical techniques may be the only way to test a market s contestability, but it will be difficult to find robust models for this. Still, global markets call for a global framework for competition policy, or at least for increased coordination among countries competition policies. Furthermore, because different industries are involved in the production and delivery of financial services, regulators within and across countries will have to coordinate how they define and assess violations of competition policy.

In some product markets, network externalities may become important for competition policy because they can create entry barriers once critical mass is reached, and market participants will have strong incentives to internalize these externalities and the associated rents. Markets involving network externalities warrant regulation to ensure access and efficient outcomes (Weinberg 1997; Shapiro and Varian 1999; Simons and Stavins 1998). As noted, network externalities are especially important in areas such as payment services and trading systems (see Table 6).

For example, automated teller machine (ATM) systems in the United States started as small, private proprietary systems, then standardized and, over time, linked up nationally without creating serious competitive concerns. In many continental European countries with concentrated banking systems, single nationwide networks with adequate access developed. But in some countries regulators had to force more open access on these networks, regulate pricing policies, limit exclusivity agreements, and overcome first-mover advantages.

Similarly, governments may need to force public access on other network services, trading systems, and electronic communication networks. And in some cases governments may have a role precisely when network externalities are difficult to internalize, as when a basic technology must be shown to be technologically feasible. For example, the Internet may not have reached critical mass as quickly as it did without early government subsidies.

Authorities have generally allowed markets and actors to proceed with little restriction, with entry in financial services by nonfinancial entities and strategic alliances between financial and nonfinancial entities. Entry by nonfinancial entities has increased competition, particularly in services traditionally provided by banks. Aggregators such as Lending Tree in the United States, Advantage Mortgage in Hong Kong (China), and DollarDEX in Singapore have increased competition and widened access in mortgage markets. New payment services, such as the Octopus card in Hong Kong (China), bypass banks and lower the costs and increase the quality of services. New entities in the brokerage business have sharply lowered commissions in many countries.

While entry by nonbanks has increased competition in financial services, the mixing of brand names, distribution networks, and financial services is leading to complex ownership and alliance structures, and extensive vertical integration could undermine competition. Such links can lead to fewer benefits for consumers when they exploit reputation or involve sunk-cost investment to reduce competition on price.[6] Mixed conglomerate structures can also challenge a basic principle of competition policy, the separation of content and carriage. Some mixed conglomerates such as a telecom company merged with a financial service provider will be able to control content and carriage and can limit access to networks by buyers of services, or by suppliers that wish to access potential customers.

As long as new entry is possible in important parts of the chain or the complete chain, vertical links may not inhibit competition. Moreover, lack of competition may not result in higher prices for financial services, but it could reduce product and process innovation. To ensure competition and innovation, restrictions may be called for on vertical or horizontal links. In considering such restrictions, authorities will have to balance many issues, including the potential risk diversification benefits of mixed conglomerates and the benefits for competition of entry by nonfinancial entities.

Securing more efficient production and delivery of financial services requires a competition framework that provides for liberal entry to and cross-border provision of financial services. A contestable system is needed for both foreign and domestic providers of financial services, including nonbanks.

Recognizing the potential gains, several countries with unsophisticated financial systems have taken an open stance toward imports of financial services. For example, in 1997 Ghana, Kenya, Malawi, and Mozambique committed to almost entirely opening their financial systems to foreign competition. For these and other countries, effective opening will require removing indirect barriers, such as harmonizing standards in many areas.

Opening to foreign competition does more than give countries access to more efficient financial services. It also allows countries particularly less developed ones to benefit from competition policies that the source country applies to financial service providers. As a result underdeveloped countries can move forward without an elaborate domestic competition policy especially important when institutional capacity is weak.

Still, some issues, particularly the possible links between network providers and financial service providers, may require attention from local policymakers. Given the potential for monopolistic behavior in markets such as telecommunications, vertical integration of financial service providers and network providers whether through ownership, strategic alliances, or otherwise can raise issues for competition policy. Many such issues are not specific to the financial sector, and arise more generally in e-commerce. But they can be important, particularly in smaller markets with only a few network providers.

Market functioning, fragmentation, and volatility

As noted, emerging markets are making greater use of global trading systems, and capital raising is increasingly moving to more liquid offshore exchanges. As a result liquidity has fallen in local exchanges especially in small economies but also in larger emerging markets. The development of local capital markets and the role of local exchanges will likely continue to change. Exchanges will increasingly demutualize, merge, and spin off functions while developing other business lines (software production and distribution to market participants, risk management services, cross-border clearing services, business

---

6 Gual (1999) suggests that competition through price and variable costs leads to less concentration and lower entry barriers relative to competition based on taking advantage of brand or reputation through investments involving sunk costs.

to business exchange development and support, and so on).

The challenges in regulating and supervising securities markets will require a new model for authorities (Box 10). Issues include the scope of regulatory oversight within and across borders, constraints to joint enforcement as more trading of emerging market securities takes place abroad, and definitions of what constitutes an exchange, an alternative trading system, an order routing system, and a brokerage operation. How should governance and ownership structures be restricted to avoid conflicts of interest as demutualization proceeds, and what self-regulating functions should be performed?

Harmonization of standards and practices

The increased ability to deliver services across borders raises issues for the harmonization of

standards and practices. First is the degree to which residents will be allowed to access financial services provided by foreign firms. While technology will provide domestic residents with more flexible access to services from anywhere such as an insurance product purchased on the Internet from a foreign financial institution the ability to do so will be determined by the rules in the country where the consumer resides.

Many countries limit the cross-border provision of financial services. They require, for example, local establishment for foreign financial institutions to be able to solicit business onshore. They also limit solicitation more implicitly through know thy customer rules that require physical registration before services can be delivered online. These limits will be harder to impose as the Internet extends its reach and as the location of providers becomes harder to pinpoint,

---

Box 10
Challenges for market regulation within and across countries

Securities market regulation confronts complex challenges when it crosses borders. Three mutually nonexclusive approaches should be considered.

One is where a country's regulator retains primary responsibility for markets, with mutual recognition of supervision. This approach would only work for countries with similar rules and would require some harmonization. Local regulators would maintain primary responsibility even when trading platforms are based offshore or when trades are primarily in foreign stocks (say, U.S. stocks traded on a European exchange). This is essentially the European approach—mutual recognition with some harmonization.

A second model is the exchange registration approach, where the domestic regulator applies the same regulations to foreign and domestic exchanges operating in the country. This could imply that exchanges are subject to multiple regulations. For example, a European-based exchange operating in the United States and Europe would be subject to U.S. and European regulations.

Finally, access providers—such as brokers that provide investors with access to foreign exchanges—could be regulated (in addition to whatever regulation applies to the exchanges). This approach does not overcome the problem that investors can get access in many ways, often with no clear jurisdictional oversight.

Whichever approach is taken, even more fundamental questions arise in harmonizing definitions of an exchange, an alternative trading system, or a broker-dealer. Furthermore, countries that are home to many companies listed and traded abroad will need to find ways to jointly enforce securities

actions. Such efforts may involve not just memorandums of understanding but also changes in legal enforcement power—including investigatory powers and secrecy statutes for financial institutions—to support active, timely, and effective cooperation.

Across and within countries there is a need to more carefully define the functions of exchanges and self-regulating organizations given the trend toward demutualization and the for-profit nature of many intermediaries. A for-profit exchange may not be subject to conflicts of interest if maintaining its reputation and service are its key sources of order flow. But in many emerging markets, exchanges have few incentives to undertake certain self-policing functions. A for-profit exchange, with the accompanying financial pressures for new shareholders, and given the increasing migration of order flow abroad, could seek to block competition through legislation or regulation. Hence it will be important to ensure competition in the provision of trading and related services.

There is also a trend toward consolidation of back-end systems and clearing custody and clearing arrangements for securities. This trend is especially evident in Europe, where Euronext (Paris, Amsterdam, and Brussels) is consolidating the provision of depository services and establishing one central clearing counterparty that will offer such services across all cash and derivative instruments traded in fixed income and equity in these three markets. A unified structure can greatly reduce risks in securities markets. But for that to happen, solvency statutes must be harmonized across countries. Proper supervision and regulation of central clearing counterparties will require more cooperation among supervisory agencies.

Source: Aggarwal 2000; *The Economist* 2001.

solicitation harder to define, and the definition of a financial service more complex. Such limits can then just become costly, distortive, and uncompetitive.

Regulators will have to decide on the best approach and timing to phase out such restrictions. A comprehensive approach would be the global equivalent to the EU approach of a single license (passport) allowing cross-border provision with home rule regulation (Key forthcoming). This process will take time to develop partly because there will be concern that regulatory and supervisory systems in some countries are not sufficient to support such a system.

Second, when allowed, cross-border provision raises the issue of which country s standards and jurisdiction apply. Because standards differ in many areas for listing requirements, insolvency arrangements, accounting standards, and the like inconsistencies can easily arise, raising transaction costs and reducing benefits. Differences can also lead to regulatory arbitrage and raise the possibility of a race to the bottom. While standards are increasingly being harmonized for example, the International Organization of Securities Commissions recently endorsed international accounting standards proposed by the International Accounting Standard Committee lar ge differences remain.

Enforcement and legal recourse across borders can also be complicated. To some extent market forces will deal with the issue of legal jurisdiction because consumers will prefer environments that provide them with the greatest certainty as has long been the case in wholesale markets, where corporations and sovereigns generally choose to issue or cross-list in a few markets. Nevertheless, as the Internet expands the access of less informed issuers and investors to cross-border services, investor protection and transparency issues may arise. The global passport approach would assign the responsibility for supervision to the home authority. But even with more harmonized standards, that may not be sufficient. Short of fully harmonized regulation and supervision, regulators may need to act within their own jurisdictions.

Closer links through technology require closer coordination in many areas. The spread of alternative trading networks across borders and the entrance of nontraditional financial service providers, for example, can create new risks. Increased use of technology and networks adds to operational risks of computer breakdowns or infiltration by hackers on a global scale. Safeguards across trading systems, within and across countries, will need to be developed. Cross-margining or ex post collateral-sharing agreements will become essential as trading goes global and involves position taking on many electronic exchanges. Even with safeguards, many new systems will have untested market stability features, and their operators may lack experience and be subject to spillovers from nonfinancial parts of the group anywhere in the world. Access of new systems to contingent financing mechanisms is unclear, especially on a global basis.

In general, the links between operators and systemic risks will become harder to understand. The Russian and Long Term Capital Management crises of 1998 surprised many. The lines between financial and other markets will become even more blurred as trading spreads through power, natural gas, and agricultural commodity contracts, risking greater spillovers from nonfinancial institutions and markets to financial markets. Going forward, firms and regulators will be pressed to respond quickly to any disruptive event anywhere in the world, potentially turning once-manageable situations into systemic crises. Risk safeguards will have to be extended within countries and on a global basis, and greater information sharing will be necessary among regulators and self-regulating organizations.

E-finance Applications—and Implications for Government

Private solutions will help countries reap many of the benefits of e-finance even when the enabling environment is imperfect. But further gains will require improving this environment. Thus e-finance calls for a review of government s role direct and indirect in the financial sector. In general, e-finance allows governments to curtail many of their direct efforts to provide financial services (for example, through development banks). But other, less direct approaches have become more attractive, such as using government infrastructure including post and telegraph offices for the private delivery of financial services.

Government's role in the financial sector is changing—and becoming less direct

Government intervention in the financial sector has generally had very poor results. Attempts to reach underserviced groups often miss their targets, are captured by special interests, and incur large fiscal costs. Government ownership of banks tends to retard financial sector development and increase the risk of financial crises (World Bank 2001; Barth, Caprio, and Levine forthcoming; La Porta, Lopez-de-Silanes, and Shleifer 2000).

E-finance can reduce the need for government intervention. The increased availability of financial services, almost regardless of a country s level of financial sector development, reduces the need for government to provide financial services or to direct intermediaries to do so. Moreover, market failures are less likely: information is more readily available and, with reforms, can be of higher quality. These improvements allow financial services to be provided more widely and make markets for trading risks and assets more complete reducing the need for government to provide financial services and to mitigate risk.

So, government s main remaining role is to enhance the enabling environment. In addition, there can be scope to improve information and increase private access to that information. For example, information on public registries for collateral could be shared more easily using new technology. Government can also make more information available, such as basic information on consumers (say, utility bills if administered by a public agency). But this more active role needs to be balanced against privacy concerns.

In addition, government can make better use of existing infrastructure and reduce duplicate infrastructure (such as branches and agencies of development banks or state banks). Here creative use of the post office network (as proposed in India and South Africa) and even telegraph offices (as proposed in Mexico) can have a major impact (Box 11).

Government s role can change dramatically in many areas where it once delivered financial services including retail payment and banking services, housing finance, insurance, nonbank financial services (factoring, leasing), storage finance, trade finance, lending to small and medium-size enterprises, and even microlending. E-finance coupled with basic reforms will allow private market participants to deliver such services far more effectively to a much wider audience with much smaller transactions, even in remote areas. The Internet slashes processing costs for providers and search and switching costs for consumers. As a result providers can market many financial services to low-income borrowers because smaller transactions still provide adequate profit. As the rest of this paper shows, many financial services are already being delivered electronically, even in emerging markets.

Smart cards provide a new way of delivering financial services

In advanced countries single and multipurpose cards are replacing or complementing other forms of payment (Box 12). In less advanced countries these cards are seen as a new way to build financial systems. Issued by private providers of financial services, such cards are used for small transactions and are often tied to payroll systems.

Over time these cards could be tied to cellular phones and other communication devices such as kiosks and be linked to other databases and financial transfers, including publicly provided social services (see Annex 4 for examples of smart card applications around the world). Cards can also be linked with public infrastructure, as between Mondex (an international electronic cash system) and South Africa s post office, so that they can be offered in remote regions. Such cards can be a far more efficient alternative to traditional development bank lending in regions such as Africa.

Box 11

Making creative use of existing public infrastructure: Post offices

In emerging markets as different as South Africa and India, efforts are under way to use publicly owned infrastructure—particularly post and telegraph offices—as conduits for delivering nonfinancial and e-finance services, and as access points for information.

South Africa's post office provides a wide variety of services, including financial services, to more than 40 million people dispersed over some 1.2 million square kilometers. Under the citizens' post office concept the agency provides telephones, fax machines, computers, Internet access, and other value added financial services through alliances with a growing number of private providers in search of appropriate distribution channels. The post office has already formed alliances with e-commerce companies such as Compuquote (offering comparative insurance and financial quotations) to provide financial services through terminals in its branches. The terminals also allow people in remote areas to access e-mail and obtain information online, such as comparative prices for inputs and crops common in rural areas. Users are certified through biometric systems (based on their fingerprints) that

allow for unique identification and registration, then assigned e-mail accounts and personal identification numbers for access. The system also allows users to pay bills for retail services (see Box 12).

India is conducting a similar experiment. The government has been investing in high-speed (DSL) Internet connections to link the country's 154,000 post office branches with 110 million savings account holders (in a country with 1 billion people). The government is also using the VSAT (satellite system) to link all the branches and to permit international money transfers—at much cheaper rates. This infrastructure will be open to multiple private providers, including providers of financial services, and promises to greatly expand access to financial services. Post offices can serve as points of origination for authentication, sources of education about social and other services, gateways to purchase retail goods, payment points for municipal and federal bills, vehicles for electronic debit card information and related transfers, points for payment of key benefits (such as pensions), and even dissemination points for essential information such as commodity prices.

Source: Glaessner, Ladekarl, and Klapper 2000; Bell and others 2001.

Box 12

Smart cards: A clever way to leapfrog?

Smart cards hold value electronically and can be used to make payments. Such cards can allow countries to leapfrog stages of financial sector development because they ease the need for costly and comprehensive financial infrastructure. Smart cards can also lower costs and reduce the need for traditional credit history checking.

Thus there is growing interest in smart cards in Africa. In 1999, 16 East and Southern African countries jointly purchased franchise rights to Mondex, an international e-cash system. The system permits the transfer of value between cards without the need to centrally record every transaction, allows for offline transactions, and reduces cash handling costs. In addition, the cards can handle multiple currencies and can be used across countries.

This initiative has inspired similar efforts elsewhere. Ghana plans to introduce a chip-based, preauthorized offline payment card—the first example of e-cash banking in West Africa—as well as other e-banking products based on smart

cards. These initiatives could allow Ghana to move from having almost no e-banking infrastructure to having full e-cash capability.

Other projects include a joint effort between Mondex and South Africa's post office (see Box 11). Using the country's 2,000 post bank counters, the project will give South Africa's most remote region its first banking services. Smart cards will enable people to set up pseudo bank accounts, with biometrics technology providing reliable identification. The e-accounts can be used, after a cardholder has paid in benefits or wages, to make payments and to set up savings pools for specific investments. South Africa's post office also takes advantage of the existing payment settlement system on behalf of the post office savings bank. It offers retail payment services such as "Pay a Bill," which allows more than a hundred accounts to be paid at post office counters—including accounts with Telkom, municipalities, mail order houses, financial institutions, and credit cards.

Source: Hitachi Research Institute 2000; Mondex 1999, 2000.

The Internet offers a new approach to housing finance

Around the world, authorities have played a big role in housing finance because of housing s importance for economic development and because of social demands for such finance. As a result many government-backed housing development banks

have been created to perform all relevant functions from loan origination to financing.

But housing finance can involve many steps from the time a house is appraised to the time all documentation has been obtained to underwrite a loan. The Internet allows for the unbundling and automation of mortgage loan processing. It can also cut search costs for consumers of mortgage services. Especially in emerging markets, many mortgage services are quite costly, and the Internet could make mortgage loan underwriting much more efficient.

Furthermore, when government development banks subsidize mortgage finance, it discourages private actors from developing ways to mitigate risks or cut transaction costs. Most of these distortions occur because authorities often do not separate the financing of mortgage loans from the subsidies being provided. Where this distinction has been made, mortgage loans are becoming more efficient, including by using the Internet. Advantage Mortgage in Hong Kong (China) and DollarDEX in Singapore are two examples of what will likely be a growing number of online providers of housing finance (Box 13). Like online brokerages, these companies are also starting to offer their services across borders. Emerging markets offer considerable potential for the electronic delivery of mortgage loans unlike some more advanced countries, where growth has been slow because housing finance systems are reasonably efficient.

In addition to originating loans, the Internet can play a role in housing markets by providing information on financing and other options to a wide spectrum of potential homeowners. Given the many steps involved in buying a home, the Internet can also slash transaction costs. For example, Internet platforms have been used to lower the cost of real estate appraisals and to secure financing. Automated loan preparation can also generate big savings (see Box 13). Finally, the clearing and information exchange functions made possible by the Internet through a business to business model applied to home buyers and sellers can provide a powerful boost for efficiency.

Insurance products are increasingly being offered online

Like housing, insurance is an industry where governments in emerging markets have provided services directly such as reinsurance, crop insurance, and support for victims of natural disasters. Such insurance is often meant to redistribute income or mitigate risks.

In countries as diverse as Korea, Mexico, the Philippines, and Singapore, insurance products are increasingly being offered electronically to consumers directly and through intermediaries, allowing different roles for government (Box 14). Most of the insurance companies offering services online allow consumers to shop for different products, using complex algorithms to ensure proper comparisons. Some companies have established business to business exchanges like those for global risk and reinsurance. The increasing penetration of insurance portals and the growing interest of major insurers in entering emerging markets using e-finance make it far less likely that governments need to directly provide insurance products as long as an enabling environment is in place.

Box 13

Mortgage finance: The impact of the Internet

Advantage Mortgage began operations as the only true specialized mortgage broker in Hong Kong (China). Over time the company has become an overall aggregator much like lendingtree.com in the United States. Advantage derives its revenue from fees paid by 15 of the biggest lenders in Hong Kong's real estate market as well as 2 lenders not supervised by the Hong Kong Monetary Authority. Advantage solicits borrowers, evaluates mortgage loan packages for presentation to borrowers, prepares all documentation required to underwrite loans and send complete loan packages to final lenders, and provides offline support on documentation. Advantage assumes no underwriting risks and does not charge borrowers for such services because prospective lenders pay all fees. Advantage is also acting as a backup underwriter for mortgage insurance given its expertise and knowledge about mortgage

borrowers. It is considering expanding to China, Korea, and Taiwan (China).

DollarDEX in Singapore is using the Internet to help financial institutions sell products, including home loans, car loans, travel insurance, and a variety of others. DollarDEX has become a kind of third-party aggregator of such products on behalf of lenders. In particular, it has developed block reverse auctions for home loans to lower the prices that consumers pay—providing a kind of aggregation and search engine service. Like Advantage, DollarDEX does not really take on credit risk, but transfers the loan files to financial institutions that then do the underwriting. The company is also targeting markets such as Hong Kong (China), Malaysia, the Philippines, Taiwan (China), and Thailand—precisely because the potential profits are higher in less developed, less efficient markets.

Source: Claessens, Glaessner, Klingebiel, 2000.

Box 14

Insurance: E-financeable?

How e-finance will affect insurance is the subject of intense debate in the industry. Many insurance companies recognize the Internet's potential as more than a marketing tool, but e-insurance applications remain limited. In part this is because most life insurance, pension products, health insurance, and commercial insurance appear to have limited suitability for sale on the Internet. Still, many firms recognize that the Internet will lower costs and improve customer service. This realization is perhaps more pronounced in some emerging markets, where traditional insurance products have had limited penetration.

In 1999 Renaissance Insurance became the first Russian insurer to go online. Clients can pay for eight different insurance policies using the company's payments system. In 2000 Ingosstrakh, Russia's largest insurance company, launched a site allowing clients to apply for insurance online. So far, however, payments must be made in the offices of Ingosstrakh. In Mexico Grupo Nacional Provincial is offering online automotive policies through a joint venture with the International Insurance Group. Consumers, agents, brokers, and insurance companies can buy insurance policies directly from a Website. Yapster.com in the Philippines has set up an online portal that offers end-to-end delivery of insurance products and services, with instant quotes available from a range of providers.

Re2Re, a Bermudas-incorporated company with offices in Hong Kong (China) and the Philippines, has developed an open exchange for global insurance risks and reinsurance capacities. Re2Re uses proprietary technology to improve reinsurance exchange between direct insurance companies, insurance brokers, reinsurance companies, and reinsurance brokers worldwide. DollarDEX is a Singaporean company that enables online consumers to compare, shop, auction, and apply for loans and insurance products from more than 30 leading financial institutions in Asia. Customers can get instant quotations based on a full comparison of features and prices, and can buy motor, travel, hospital, home, personal, long-term care, and other insurance. DollarDEX recently pioneered the first fully online life insurance product, M@xivalue, which enables healthy applicants to get instant approval. Prudential Insurance of the United States plans to introduce new Web-based investment products in Korea, Mexico, and Taiwan (China). Its move, complemented by a greater brick-and-mortar presence, is part of efforts to offer online insurance products globally.

In March 2000 the first insurance Website was launched in China. Wangxian delivers insurance documents to policyholders and allows customers to use credit cards to purchase insurance. Sohu.com, a major Web portal, and Taikang Online, a major insurer, followed the same trend in 2001. The two companies offer online insurance services to clients, agents, and other insurance companies.

Source: See bibliographical note.

An e-revolution is occurring in factoring, leasing, storage finance, and trade finance

Factoring, leasing, storage finance, supplier credit, and trade finance are well-established financial services. Companies use these techniques to obtain finance by pledging receivables, leasing machinery or other financial or nonfinancial assets, pledging warehouse receipts to finance storage of goods in warehouses, and pledging actual or expected trade-related receipts. These forms of finance are important in many emerging markets especially where banking systems are under stress and standard means of contract enforcement are deficient. E-finance can improve the delivery of these services and substantially lower transaction costs given the often paper-intensive documentation required for these services.

Factoring and leasing

New technology has lowered the cost and increased the availability and ease of transferring information. This development has increased lender and client opportunities for factoring, which is the sale of accounts receivable, and leasing, which are loans collateralized by assets such as accounts receivable and inventory, as well as other forms of asset-based lending. Electronic transmission of sales and receipts allows real-time information exchange, increases security, enables immediate credit decisions, and lowers transaction costs. Lenders can continuously access firms ledgers to track changes in outstanding receivables as inventory is sold and receivables are collected, lowering the transaction costs for clients. New factoring companies offering online applications and more transparent rates have increased competition and reduced fees even further. But as with other electronic transactions, more secure technology should be developed to prevent fraud and to extend laws to cover electronic sales of receivables.

Storage finance

Storage finance is an area where governments in many emerging markets have played a large role by providing storage for agricultural commodities as in India and by purchasing physical stocks on grounds of security as in African and to a lesser extent Asian and Latin American countries. E-finance offers interesting possibilities for storage finance. The ability to track commodities being stored, to uniquely define storage certificates, and to keep warehouse receipts electronically can facilitate the provision of credit against stored goods for farmers, exporters, and processing companies. In India and Mexico Internet platforms are being developed to trade and pledge electronic warehouse receipts. These developments will reduce the need for government to purchase commodities for stockpiling and to provide financing to farmers.

Trade finance

Trade finance is another area where governments have provided credit to exporters and importers, often through development banks. New technology will allow letters of credit, bills of lading, and other documents associated with trade finance to be dematerialized and tracked electronically, resulting in large savings. Bolero.net, a joint venture between the Society for Worldwide Interbank Financial Telecommunications, commercial banks, freight forwarders, and shipping companies, is one of the first platforms to completely automate trade finance, reducing handling time and delays caused by improper documentation. This and other

mechanisms will also allow smaller transactions, increasing access to trade finance for smaller businesses and so expanding the volume of trade financed. Electronic trade finance will require adequate security arrangements as well as a framework for using electronic signatures.

Small and medium-size enterprises can secure finance electronically

Lending to small and medium-size enterprises is yet another area where e-finance can obviate the need for direct government intervention. Small and medium-size enterprises are major sources of growth and employment, and authorities around the world are constantly evaluating how best to ensure their access to finance including through existing or even new government-owned development banks. But development banks have often proven to be the wrong approach (Barth, Caprio, and Levine forthcoming; La Porta, Lopez-de-Silanes, and Shleifer 2000).

Instead, governments need to provide the infrastructure and platforms needed for private entities to offer such finance electronically including through public infrastructure such as post offices. E-finance for small and medium-size enterprises is already a reality in many parts of the world; SMEloan in Hong Kong (China) and Pride

---

Box 15

E-finance for small and medium-size enterprises

SMEloan Hong Kong Limited (known as SMEloan) has reengineered the commercial lending process using the Internet and has become Hong Kong's (China) leading provider of online financing for small and medium-size enterprises. SMEloan conducts most of its lending on the Internet and manages credit risk using a Web-based risk management model. In October 2000 SMEloan closed a HK$600 million (about US$75 million) financing facility with a group of banks, a first for a startup e-finance company in Asia. The facility will enable SMEloan to expand its current customer base of 200 small and medium-size enterprises to well over 1,000 by mid-2002.

Pride Africa is a financial institution that provides access to credit to more than 80,000 small-scale entrepreneurs in Kenya, Malawi, Tanzania, Uganda, and Zambia. Pride Africa has created DrumNet, a virtual network linking clients to markets, information, and services. Through its network of microlending branches and information kiosks, Pride Africa's clients will have access to wholesale supplies and services, advertising, and partnership and association building opportunities. To integrate

microentrepreneurs with the formal financial sector, Pride Africa created Sunlink Cashpoints. Sunlink clients have smart cards that provide teller access, loan authorization, and client identification, helping to establish credit ratings—and so facilitating access by small and medium-size enterprises to other financial services.

Major financial conglomerates with worldwide operations are also entering the market for small and medium-size enterprises. In 1999 Citigroup created CitiBusiness, a business group that specializes in financial services for such enterprises. In 2000 it launched the CitiBusiness Platinum Select Master Card, which in addition to providing credit gives access to various services—including information on building a Website, setting up an employee benefits program, and so on. In early 2001 Citigroup introduced CitiBusiness Direct, a comprehensive Internet banking program, to small and medium-size enterprises in the Czech Republic, Hungary, and India. In India CitiBusiness accounts for 15 percent of Citigroup's corporate bank business, and counts 5,000 small and medium-size enterprises among its clients.

Source: See bibliographical note.

Africa show what is possible (Box 15). Pride Africa s DrumNet, a network linking small clients in several African countries to markets, information, and services, may be replicable. Large financial conglomerates are also starting to target small and medium-size enterprises because the lower transaction costs made possible by e-finance make this market attractive.

New technology can increase access to microfinance

Governments often intervene in microfinance through direct programs that mix financing with subsidies. As with lending for small and medium-size enterprises, the Internet and other new technology will further weaken the case for such direct intervention. Whether it is the development of an Internet-only bank that delivers services to the urban poor or the use of smart cards and even cellular phones to reduce processing time for microloans (Box 16), technology can dramatically lower the costs of delivering financial services to such borrowers increasing access. In addition, to the extent that such activities are automated and

information about customers is pooled and provided to credit bureaus, there can be a natural move by clients to more formal methods of finance.

Changes in securities markets offer chances for faster development

E-finance and new technology will also allow for big changes in the operation of payments systems and other middle- and back-office functions for financial service providers as well as for the faster development of an entire communications network backbone. Hong Kong (China), Malaysia, and Singapore are trying to interconnect all financial service providers into financial nets that will allow straight-through processing, payment versus payment, significantly lower costs, and better risk management (Box 17). Because much of the infrastructure for securities markets is starting to operate on a for-profit basis and because monopolies are disappearing (as in clearing and settlement systems), governments will increasingly need to set the overall framework for connecting these systems and assess the risks in doing so, rather than regulate or own specific infrastructure components.

Box 16

Microfinance and e-finance—a viable match?

Access, cost, and technical expertise are the main factors hindering the use of information and communications technology by microfinance institutions. Yet new technology can not only transform systems for delivering microcredit to the poor, it can also facilitate the microfinance business itself.

In 1993 South Africa's Standard Bank created an affiliate, E Bank, to deliver basic bank services to the urban poor. Using modified automated teller machines (ATMs), E Bank provides a package of financial services, including payment services and savings accounts, designed for low-income clients. By rethinking the needs of basic bank customers, E Bank was able to bundle services valued by poor clients while covering costs with low overall fees. In Nigeria, Gemcard plans to give smart cards to poor citizens so that they can participate in a microcredit scheme involving local banks. Bank services will be provided by mobile vans that use facial biometrics to identify customers. The project aims to encourage good banking habits among the poor and to collect funds from the informal sector.

ACCIÓN International, one of the world's leading microfinance organizations, is using handheld computers to cut the time and cost of making microloans. Loan officers record all loan data using Palm Pilots, which frees them from carrying burdensome equipment when visiting clients. Including the time it takes to record data and upload it back at the office, it takes less than an hour to process a loan. New software will allow

loan officers to record client data, take applications, and make loan calculations on the spot.

PlaNet Finance, launched in 1999, aims to share knowledge among microfinance institutions and promote local initiatives. PlaNet Finance has created PlaNet Fund to provide microfinance institutions with services like loans, guarantees, joint funding, and bond purchases. For example, a carpenter in Bolivia who needed new tools applied to a local microfinance institution for a loan, but the institution could not provide the funds. So the microfinance institution made an Internet appeal to PlaNet Fund, combining the applications of several craftsmen. A specialist on Bolivia examined the case in La Paz, Peru, and gave his approval to PlaNet Fund, which quickly disbursed the loan.

Similar to the PlaNet Finance concept, the United Nations Conference on Trade and Development has created the Virtual Microfinance Market, an information exchange designed to facilitate interactions between microfinance institutions, private investors, governments, and other participants in the microfinance market. The Virtual Microfinance Market is aimed at creating sustainable market links between commercial investors and microenterprises in developing countries, and is expected to permit the investment (using commercial terms) of millions of dollars at the grassroots level and the creation of thousand of jobs.

Source: See bibliographical note.

Box 17

FinNet: Toward a paperless infrastructure backbone for financial services

Hong Kong (China), along with some other economies, has been modernizing its financial network infrastructure to enhance its status as a financial center and become one of Asia's most convenient centers for business to business commerce. Governed by a public-private partnership, a financial network, FinNet, will be established (see Figure). FinNet will be a secure, open, scalable, and high-performance community network interconnecting all types of financial services and all financial markets and institutions in Hong Kong (China). This includes all securities, derivatives, banking, and insurance activities; all licensed financial entities and key government agencies (such as regulatory agencies); law firms; independent mortgage brokers and insurance companies; independent financial planners; and even overseas systems if they meet certain standards. FinNet will allow straight-through processing of all functions related to financial transactions, from the front end to the back end. In addition, it will permit real-time delivery versus payment and payment versus payment.

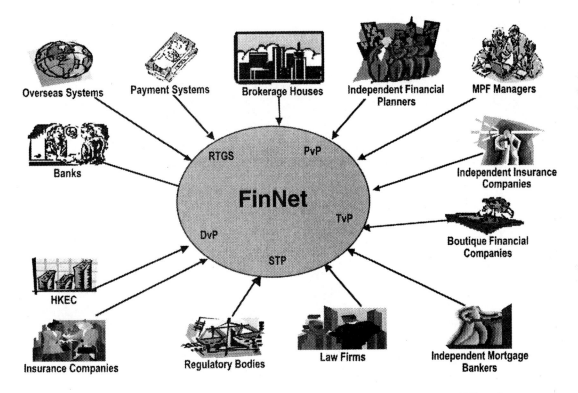

DvP = delivery versus payment; RTGS = real time gross settlement system; PvP = payment versus payment; TvP = trade versus payment; STP = straight through processing; MPF=mutual portfolio funds; HKEC = Hong Kong exchanges

Source: Hong Kong Monetary Authority.

Annex 1: Data Sources and Methodology for the Projections

Data sources for Table 1

The share of online banking customers is from various sources. Data for Belgium, Denmark, France, Italy, the Netherlands, Norway, Portugal, Spain, Sweden, the United Kingdom, and the United States were furnished by DataMonitor for 1999. Data for Australia, the Czech Republic, Germany, Hong Kong (China), Hungary, Mexico, and Poland were furnished by their central banks for 1999. Data for Argentina, Brazil, Finland, and Singapore were provided by Credit Suisse in 1998. Data for India was provided by Netsense for 2000.

The share of online brokerage customers is from various sources. Data for Belgium, Denmark, France, Germany, Italy, the Netherlands, Norway, Portugal, Spain, Sweden, the United Kingdom, and the United States were provided by DataMonitor for 1999. Data for Japan was furnished by Monex for 2000. Data for Australia, China, the Czech Republic, Hong Kong (China), Korea, and Mexico were furnished by their central banks for 2000. Data for Singapore was furnished by TD Waterhouse for 2000. Data for India was furnished by Netsense for 2000, and data for Brazil by E-Trade for 2000.

Business environment rankings were furnished by the Economist Intelligence Unit Country Forecast. The rankings cover 60 countries, and have been used in other contexts to predict levels of foreign direct investment.

Methodology for the projections

The projected takeoff years in Table 4 are based on the data on online banking from Table 1. These are typically 2000 data for European countries and end-1999 data for the United States. The takeoff year is based on a pattern of penetration that can best be described as an S-curve. The shape of the S-curve is determined by the penetration rate at which takeoff occurs, the final level of saturation, and the rate of hyper growth. The final level of saturation is set at 100 percent. The rate of hyper growth is set at a value such that it would take 10 years after takeoff to reach full saturation. The current penetration level for each industrial country is then matched to the one implied by an S-curve. The S-curve chosen then implies a certain date at which hyper growth will start (or has already started if the current penetration level is higher than the penetration rate at which takeoff occurs).

These (derived) hyper growth takeoff dates for the 16 industrial countries were used in conjunction with an ordinary least squares regression to find the relationship between takeoff dates (dependent variable) and the EIU business environment rankings and connectivity indexes (independent variables, as reported in Tables 1 and 4). For online banking, the connectivity index is a more important explanatory variable than the business environment ranking. Specifically, the regression results are: takeoff $= 2014 - 1.71 *$ Conn, with $R2 = 0.397$. For online brokerage, both the business environment ranking and connectivity index are important explanatory factors. Specifically, the regression results are: takeoff $= 2027.2 - 2.16 *$ BusEnv $- 1.49 *$ Conn, with $R2 = 0.8$. Using these two regression results, the other countries business environment ranking and connectivity index are used to project the takeoff dates for banking and brokerage for each country.

These projected takeoff dates and the corresponding S-curves imply certain projected shares of online banking and brokerage customers for each year in each industrial country and emerging market. We next use assumptions on net interest margins and brokerage revenues for traditional and online operations to project the future net interest margin and brokerage revenues given these shares of online activities in each country in each year. To do so, we need an assumption of the revenues generated from online transactions. Specifically, we assume that net interest income as a share of banking assets mar gins for online banking services would be 1.6 percentage points, which is below average for banking margins in most countries. While there are significant upfront costs, it is realistic to expect that in the medium term the online costs for delivering banking services will be much lower than current costs at least as low as those experienced by today s most Internet-savvy banks. Since Nordic counties have seen the most e-finance, their current cost structure may be indicative of a cost structure under fully electronic financial service provision. In 1997/98 margins in Nordic countries were 1.6 percentage points or less.

Revenues for banks from providing traditional services in a fully e-finance world may be even lower since Nordic (and other) banks have not yet completed their transformation to a more e-finance world. Nordic, Dutch and other banks, for example, are still reducing branches and staff considerably (see the *Financial Stability Report* of RiksBank, November 2000). As such, their current cost structures might be higher than their long-run cost structure. The 1.6 percentage point margin, for example, is definitely higher than the marginal costs of providing e-finance services, which are estimated to be only a few cents per transaction, compared with about $1 for a branch transaction and 50 cents for an automated teller machine. On the other hand, recent experience has shown that banks may need a brick and clicks approach, which would involve higher overall costs than the marginal costs of providing a transaction online. On balance, the current revenues of Swedish banks may represent a good but low estimate of the long-run overall cost advantages of e-finance.

For brokerage revenues, we assume that online-only revenues are about 25 percent of normal brokerage revenues. This share is still less than the drop in commissions in markets like the United States since the introduction of online brokerage. Again, the marginal costs of online-only provision are much lower than those of traditional sources. The competition already seen for this type of financial service implies that much of the cost savings can be expected to be passed on to consumers. In Korea, for example, online-only brokerage services have been provided for free by some competitors. Again, a bricks and clicks approach is likely necessary, so the 25 percent projection might represent a balanced estimate of the long-run overall cost advantages of e-brokering.

Projections are undertaken using the margins and brokerage revenues prevailing in each country with 1997 as the starting point. We use 1997 because that year was less affected by the introduction of e-finance. We project new margins and revenues in each year in each country until 2010 given the specific projected shares of online banking and brokerage. This projection methodology assumes that incumbent financial institutions have to lower their margins and fees to the online-only costs in line with the projected shares of online banking and brokerage. Thus the projection assumes that the lower cost structures of online banking are being passed on to consumers in the form of lower margins and brokerage fees. This assumption is consistent with a model of strong competition among financial institutions and relative to new entrants.

Annex 2: Recent Reports by International E-finance Working Groups

Since early 2000 international agencies have established a variety of working groups to study e-commerce and e-finance (see Table A2-1). This Annex provides a brief synopsis of these groups reports, drawing largely on official documents. Where possible, Website links are provided.

Ongoing and recent work on sound financial systems

- The Basel Committee on Banking Supervision (BCBS) is reviewing developments in electronic banking in G-10 countries. In October 2000 the BCBS Working Group on Electronic Banking released its Phase 1 Report and White Papers, which identified four areas for future work: developing guiding principles for prudent risk management of e-banking activities, consideration of cross-border issues, promoting international cooperation, and encouraging and facilitating supervisory training programs. The group issued a report on risk management principles for e-banking in May 2001. (www.bis.org)
- The World Bank is reviewing the policy implications for financial sector development of changes in financial services, markets, and institutions driven by globalization and technological advances. (www.worldbank.org)
- The Financial Action Task Force is identifying the vulnerability of Internet banking to money laundering specifically , how online banking, electronic cash, and smart cards can facilitate it. (www.oecd.org/fatf)
- The International Organization of Securities Commissions is developing a follow-up report to the 1998 Internet Task Force Report laying out further principles for securities regulation. (www.iosco.org)
- The International Association of Insurance Supervisors (IAIS) is reviewing developments in Internet-based insurance activities. There will be a detailed discussion on supervisory issues and subsequent standard setting. Principles on the supervision of insurance activities on the Internet were adopted at the IAIS 2000 annual meeting. (www.iaisweb.org)
- The Committee on the Global Financial System is assessing electronic trading in financial markets and studying its implications for financial stability. A recent report on the implications of electronic trading examined how electronic trading systems function in wholesale financial markets. (www.bis.org)
- The Committee on Payment and Systems Settlement is to study developments in Internet payment methods. It recently issued a report on clearing and settlement arrangements for retail payments in selected countries. (www.bis.org)
- The Organisation for Economic Co-operation and Development is to review the impact of e-finance on public debt management. At a November 2000 meeting the working group discussed the impact of electronic systems on sovereign debt markets, the issuance of government debt securities, and the future of primary dealer systems.

Electronic Banking Group initiatives and output

The Basel Committee established the Electronic Banking Group (EBG) in 1999 to focus on:
- Developing guiding principles for the prudent risk management of e-banking services.
- Identifying where and if existing Basel Committee guidance needs to be adapted to facilitate the sound supervision of cross-border e-banking activities.

Table A2-1

Current e-finance initiatives by international bodies

International body	Protection of privacy and personal data	Secure infrastructure: authentication and certification	Consumer protection	Commercial law	Taxation	Electronic payment and movement of goods
BIS						●
IEC		●				
ILO	●					
ISO		●				
ITC						
ITU	●	●	●	●		●
UN/CEFACT		●		●		
UNCTAD				●		●
UNESCO	●	●	●	●		
UNICITRAL		●	●	●		●
UPU	●	●	●			●
World Bank		●		●	●	●
WCO		●				●
WIPO				●		
WTO	●					●

International body	Trade facilitation and market access	Intellectual property	Internet governance	Standards	Economic and social impacts	Small and medium-size enterprises
BIS						●
IEC		●				
ILO	●					
ISO		●				
ITC						
ITU	●	●	●	●		●
UN/CEFACT		●		●		
UNCTAD				●		●
UNESCO	●	●	●	●		
UNICITRAL		●	●	●		●
UPU	●	●	●			●
World Bank		●		●	●	●
WCO		●				●
WIPO				●		
WTO	●					●

Source: OECD Emerging Market Economy Forum on Electronic Commerce, Dubai U.A.E., 16 January 2001.

■ Promoting cooperative and international efforts within the banking industry and between the public and private sectors to identify e-banking risks and sound practices to deal with them.

■ Encouraging and facilitating the exchange of supervisor e-banking training programs and materials being developed by bank supervisors.

Since e-banking is based on technology designed to expand the virtual geographic reach of banks and customers without necessarily requiring a similar physical expansion, market expansion can extend beyond national borders, which significantly increases cross-border cooperation challenges for bank supervisors. Adapting Basel Committee guidance to address e-banking issues is therefore a principal goal of the EBG.

Specific cross-border risk factors raised by e-banking include:

■ The potential ease and speed with which a bank located anywhere in the world can conduct activities with customers over interconnected electronic networks in countries where the bank is not licensed or supervised.

■ The potential ability of a bank or nonbank to use the Internet to cross borders and to seamlessly link banking activities that have typically been subject to supervision with nonbanking activities that might be unsupervised by any financial market authority.

■ The practical difficulties faced by national authorities wishing to monitor or control local access to e-banking sites originating in other jurisdictions without the cooperation of home country authorities.

Recent EBG surveys of supervisors and bankers in G-10 countries cite trends and issues that could affect bank risk profiles:

■ A significant increase in competition in the electronic financial services industry as both banking and nonbanking firms rapidly introduce new products and services.

■ Rapid technological improvements in telecommunications and computer hardware and software enabling greater speed in processing transactions.

■ Bank management and staff often lack expertise in technology and e-banking risk issues.

■ Greater reliance on outsourcing to third-party service providers, and a proliferation of new alliances and joint ventures with nonfinancial firms.

■ Greater demand for global infrastructure for technology that is scaleable, flexible, and interoperable, both within and across enterprises that can ensure the security, integrity, and availability of information and services.

■ Increased potential for fraud due to the absence of standard business practices for customer verification and authentication on open networks like the Internet.

■ Legal and regulatory ambiguity and uncertainty with respect to the application and jurisdiction of current laws and regulations relative to evolving e-banking activities.

■ The collection, storage, and frequent sharing of significant quantities of customer data can lead to customer privacy issues that potentially create prudential risks for banks.

■ Questions regarding the effectiveness and efficiency of online disclosures.

Although bank supervisors agree that the supervisory principles of traditional banking are applicable to e-banking, the amalgam of changes in technology and the degree of dependence exhibited by banks on service providers and technological distributors mutate and magnify the typical levels of risk.

Following this work, the EBG issued 14 principles for managing risk in e-banking; see Box 9 in the main text. (The full text of the group s reports can be found at www.bis.org/publ/bcbs76.htm and www.bis.org/publ/bcbs82.htm) These principles fall into three categories: effective board and management oversight, security risk issues, and reputation risk issues. Banking institutions and their supervisors should consider these principles when formulating risk management policies and processes for e-banking activities.

Implications of electronic trading in financial markets

The Committee on Global Financial Systems (CGFS) was established in 1999. Previously known as the Euro-Currency Standing Committee, the CGFS s current mandate is to analyze the functioning of international interbank markets, financial derivatives, and the systemic consequences of standard management practices. This working group took a preliminary look at the possible implications of electronic trading platforms for the functioning of global markets. It issued a report in January 2001 available at http://www.bis.org/publ/cgfs16.pdf. The following are excerpts from the report.

Electronic trading (ET) systems are systems that provide some or all of the following services: electronic order routing (the delivery of orders from users to the execution of the system), automated trade execution (the transformation of orders into trades) and post-trade information (transaction price and volume data). Electronic systems differ from traditional markets in several respects. ET is both location-neutral and allows continuous multilateral interaction. Consequently, ET systems facilitate cross-border alliances and mergers between trading systems to a greater extent than traditional markets. ET is scalable. ET is integrated. ET potentially allows straight through processing (STP), i.e. the seamless integration of the different parts of the trading process, starting from displaying pre-trade information and ending with risk management.

Electronic systems are used for trading in financial markets worldwide. ET has become the dominant method in the inter-dealer foreign exchange market and is moving into preeminent position within the inter-dealer fixed-income market. At this stage, however, ET has not made a significant showing within the OTC derivatives market. The counterparty credit risk involved in these instruments is an important reason for its limited penetration. In general ET is not widely accepted within markets wherein this type of risk is prevalent. Only in systems that have been altered to, for example, incorporate a set of limits is the counterparty credit risk effectively managed.

ET is changing market structures. The impact on market structure with regard to transparency and efficiency is vital to comprehension of the ramifications of this modern phenomenon. In the inter-dealer market, trading is moving from bilateral OTC relationships towards a marketplace with a more centralized price discovery and transparency. The foreign exchange market is being transformed, in this manner, at a significantly greater rate than the fixed-income markets wherein there are several competing systems. The role of voice booking and direct dealing between dealers is diminishing. The current market structure is one wherein many different trading mechanisms coexist. A full transformation is expected to occur to a fairly centralized and open network allowing all market participants to transact directly with each other.

Another factor lies in the contestability of the electronic market. Although ET is associated with low variable costs, entry costs may be high if fixed costs for the creation of the IT infrastructure are taken into account. First mover advantages and network externalities may make it difficult to attract business away form established systems. Liquidity does not move easily form one platform to another. Although ET makes markets more transparent, it has been noted that full disclosure of trading information does not always lead to better market functioning.

Liquidity is not expected to suffer from the introduction of ET nor is the fragmentation of markets expected to profoundly affect the cost of arbitrage. But, ET does introduce new risks. The extent to which ET systems are designed to cope with counterparty credit risk may affect their use in times of stress. ET has the potential to improve the operational efficiency of individual firms, but it also increases the dependency on these systems the design of these systems, their robustness and their contingency plans therefore deserve careful attention from both system providers and the authorities. ET is lowering transaction costs but also raising the issue of breakdown. One example would be the automated execution by systems with pricing engines. These automated systems will need human intervention and whether or not this intervention will be possible, in a timely manner, remains to be seen.

Supervision of insurance activities on the Internet

Electronic commerce presents the insurance industry with new challenges. Whereas the number of cross-border transactions will increase and insurance costs and inefficiencies will decline, the protection of policyholders becomes more difficult. In September 2000 the International Association of Insurance Supervisors issued a paper on Internet insurance activities (available at www.iaisweb.org. The paper proposes an environment for supervising insurance activities on the Internet that aims at ensuring relevant information is available to consumers, insurers, and insurance supervisors through a common set of principles. The paper proposes that insurance activities on the Internet be guided by three principles.

- *Principle 1: consistency of approach.* The supervisory approach to insurance activities on the Internet should be consistent with that applied to insurance activities through other media.
- *Principle 2: transparency and disclosure.* Insurance supervisors should require insurers and intermediaries over whom they exercise jurisdiction to ensure that the principles of transparency and disclosure applied to Internet insurance activities are equivalent to those applied to insurance activities though other media.
- *Principle 3: effective supervision of Internet activities based on cooperation.* Supervisors should cooperate with one another, as necessary, in supervising insurance activities on the Internet.

Securities activity on the Internet

In September 1998 the International Organization of Securities Commissions issued a report on securities activities on the Internet (available at www.iosco.org/docs-public/1998-internet_security.html). The report highlights how the Internet presents new challenges for securities regulators and self-regulating organizations (SROs). Electronic communication and interactivity does not coincide within the parameters of statutes, regulations, and directives originally intended for a telephone- and paper-based environment, thus creating possible regulatory burdens or unintended regulatory gaps. The report addresses the regulatory and enforcement issues posed by securities activities conducted over the Internet; the following excerpts are drawn from the report.

Key recommendations

Application of domestic regulatory requirements to securities activities on the Internet

Offers and advertisements

1. Regulators and SROs should provide guidance to alert market participants and markets as to how their existing registration, licensing and other regulatory requirements apply to offers and advertisements conducted on the Internet and alert them to the possibility that other jurisdictions likewise may impose other requirements.
2. Regulators should amend, or seek to have the relevant authorities or legislative bodies amend, specific requirements when appropriate to accommodate and ensure appropriate regulatory coverage of the Internet environment.
3. General antifraud provisions should apply to all offers and advertisements involving securities or financial services, regardless of the medium and regardless of whether a regulator or SRO is involved in approving the offer or advertisement.
4. Regulators and, where appropriate, SROs should strengthen surveillance of Internet advertising and offerings for unauthorized or fraudulent activities.

Delivery of disclosure documents and other information

5. Regulators should ensure that issuers who use the Internet to communicate with and send offering material to shareholders and potential investors provide the same disclosure about their operations, financial condition and securities that would be provided in a paper-based medium, so that investors can evaluate the risk and value of investing in the issuer.
6. Regulators should provide guidance for the financial service industry on the use of the Internet to satisfy their obligation to deliver disclosure documents. Regulators should permit the financial service industry to deliver disclosure documents electronically when an investor has given an informed consent to this form of delivery.

Communications and customer orders

8. Regulators should require that financial service providers continue to satisfy suitability and general conduct requirements when transacting business over the Internet.
9. Regulators should require that financial service providers ensure that their computer networks have sufficient operational integrity (security, reliability, capacity, backup systems and alternative means of communication) and that they have adequate personnel to handle Internet communications, including trading instructions.
10. Regulators should consider requiring financial service providers to develop written procedures for the review of incoming and outgoing electronic correspondence between employees and the public relating to the financial service provider s securities business.
11. Regulators should clarify if, and under what circumstances, the use of authentication technologies will be allowed and when manual signatures will be required.

Recordkeeping
12. Recordkeeping requirements applicable to financial service providers should apply to Internet transactions.
13. Record keeping policies and requirements should address e-mail communications that relate to the securities business of a financial service provider.

Exercise of regulatory authority over cross-border securities activities on the Internet

15. If an issuer s or financial service provider s offer or sales activities over the Internet occur within a regulator s jurisdiction, or if the issuer s or financial service provider s offshore activities, in fact, have a significant effect upon residents or markets in the regulator s jurisdiction, a regulator may impose its regulatory requirements (e.g., licensing and registration requirements) on such activities.
16. Regulators should examine the following factors in determining whether to assert regulatory authority over an offer of securities or financial services on the Internet. Factors that may support the assertion of regulatory authority include:
    ¥   It is evident that information is targeted to residents of the regulator s jurisdiction.
    ¥   The issuer or financial service provider accepts purchases from or provides services to residents of the regulator s jurisdiction (unless made pursuant to an exemption or under circumstances that may exclude a public offering).
    ¥   The issuer or financial service provider uses e-mail or other media to push the information to residents of the regulator s jurisdiction.

Use of the Internet to foster investor education and transparency

17. Regulators and SROs should include use of the Internet in educating investors and providing guidance to the securities industry.
18. Regulators and SROs should educate investors about securities fraud on the Internet by providing information about possible fraudulent activities. For example, regulators and SROs could use their Websites to post warnings regarding false or misleading offerings or advertisements.
19. Regulators, SROs, and organized markets should consider using their Websites to provide current and potential investors with access to information about their institutions, including current laws, regulations, by-laws and governance procedures.
20. Regulators, SROs, and organized markets should facilitate investor access to corporate and market information by developing electronic databases for reports and legally required disclosure documents, and making the information publicly available on their Websites.
21. Regulators and SROs should strengthen surveillance of Internet activities by routinely monitoring for unauthorized or fraudulent activities.
22. Regulators and SROs should have staff sufficiently trained in current techniques for conducting surveillance on the Internet.
23. Regulators should assist one another by exchanging details about techniques for monitoring Internet advertising, offers of securities or financial services that may contain false or misleading information, and by sharing expertise

with regulators who have limited experience in this area.

International Telecommunication Union

In 1999 the International Telecommunication Union (ITU) Council endorsed new initiatives for the Union to promote the growth of electronic commerce. The new initiatives program includes strategic planning workshops, telecommunications case studies, Internet policy, and Web publishing. Presently, the ITU serves as a forum to address policy issues related to electronic commerce in developing countries. In the program s first phase, during 1999-2000, three workshops were held. At its 2000 session the ITU Council endorsed the continuation of the program and approved guidelines for the strategic planning workshops. Broadband and 3G mobile will be the subjects of the next two workshops, to be held in 2001. In 2001 the World Telecommunication Policy Forum on IP telephony will examine challenges for developing countries, including skill shortages related to IP technology, and will likely issue an opinion on human resource development issues. Further information is available at: http://www.itu.int/itudoc/gs/subscirc/itu-d/(245-01).html

United Nations Commission on International Trade Law

In December 2000 the Working Group on Electronic Commerce of the United Nations Commission on International Trade Law (UNCITRAL) issued a study on transferable bills of lading in an electronic environment (available at www.uncitral.org/en-index.htm). The study found that:

- Developing electronic equivalents of traditional, mainly paper-based, methods for transferring or creating rights in tangible goods or intangible property may face serious obstacles where the law requires physical delivery of goods or paper documents for the purpose of transferring property or perfecting security interests in such goods or in the rights represented by the document. The problem presented by electronic commerce is how to provide a guarantee of uniqueness equivalent to possession of a document of title or negotiable instrument.
- Modern technology makes it possible to electronically transmit information down a chain of parties. The same process could conceivably be used by any of the parties to renounces its title in favor of another person, thus amounting to an endorsement of the instrument. It is true that no electronic message can be the very same as another. But so long as it is technically possible for a message to be replicated exactly and sent to someone else with no possibility of detection, there could be no guarantee of singularity.
- Electronic equivalents of paper-based negotiability should rely on central registry systems in which a central entity manages the transfer of titles between parties. Harmonized rules are needed to support the development of such systems, which can be grouped into three categories:
  1. *Government registries.* An agency of the state records transfers as public records and may authenticate or certify such transfers, as in the case of electronic registration of real estate in Canada.
  2. *Central registries.* These can be established where a commercial group conducts its transactions over a private network (such as SWIFT) that is accessible only to its members.

3. *Private registries*. These registries are conducted over open or semi-open networks, where the issuer of the document, its agent, or a trusted third party administers the transfer or negotiation process.

Related efforts include:

■ *Conflict of law issues*. In January 2001 the Secretary General of the Hague Conference convened a conference that examined the possibility of preparing and adopting, through a fast-track procedure, a new instrument dealing with the law applicable to the proprietary aspects of collateral transactions effected through indirect holding systems.

■ *Substantive law issues*. The UNCITRAL Secretariat is preparing a study on legal problems in secured credit law, including security interests in investment securities. Issues more specifically related to electronic communication such as conditions for cross-border recognition of records, standards of trustworthiness, or registry keepers and certification service providers and liability are inseparable from policy concerns on matters such as capital market regulation, interbank settlements, and monetary policy. The working group, in cooperation with the Comite Maritime International (CMI), is conducting a broad investigation of legal issues arising from the gaps left by international laws and international conventions on the international carriage of goods by sea.

Annex 3: Types of Online Trading Systems

E-trading in fixed-income securities

Online trading in fixed-income securities started in 1998 with TradeWeb, the first online bond market. Since then a highly fragmented industry has developed in which different online trading systems (platforms) compete with each other and with traditional trading systems. Intense competition has resulted in a transition toward systems that are able to attract greater liquidity to their platforms. Market participants expect this transition to be toward more centralized, open architecture that provides multiproduct coverage and wider access to investors.

Online trading systems can be divided into categories according to the trading model used, the ownership structure of the systems, the sources of prices for securities, the customer base, and coverage and products. This annex summarizes these five categories and gives some examples.

Trading model

- *Auction trading platforms.* This model allows online auctions of primary issues of fixed-income securities. The issuing party posts the details of the security offering on an auction trading platform and collects bids from investors. The offering is then automatically awarded to the best price or lowest yield bidders. Certain platforms (such as the Bloomberg secondary market auction system) also enable auctions for secondary market offerings by institutional investors. While electronic auction trading enables disintermediation in primary markets, most issuers still rely on the other services by intermediaries, such as underwriting (ensuring the sale of a security) and market making in secondary markets. Examples of auction trading systems include TreasuryDirect (for trading Treasury bills and bonds), ValuBond (for primary and secondary offerings of fixed-income securities), and MuniAuction (for online auctions of municipal securities).
- *Inquiry-based systems.* This trading model enables investors to get executable prices from multiple dealers for their inquiries to buy or sell a certain amount of securities. These systems are also able to collect information on the types and amounts of trades by large institutional investors information that is not lar gely accessible to retail investors, but instead is available only to dealers. The largest inquiry-based online trading system is TradeWeb, a multidealer consortium formed by 14 of the biggest dealers in the market.
- *Cross-matching (open architecture, exchange-based) systems.* This trading system automatically matches the bid and ask prices submitted by institutional investors and dealers. By allowing traders to get prices from many dealers and trade in large amounts anonymously, eliminating the need for intermediaries, cross-matching systems capture all the advantages of increased liquidity and more efficient execution. Such systems allow participants to see a great portion or all of the order book (by type of order). This trading model is used by online trading platforms such as Apogean Technology, Currenex, and BondBook.

Ownership structure

- *Investment banks.* The emergence of online trading has been a significant threat for investment banks, lowering the barriers to entry in the industry. This development has challenged the hold that investment banks have in this market. In response, investment banks have moved toward creating proprietary online trading platforms. Examples include Web.ET (www.gs.com/) by Goldman Sachs, PrimeTrade (www.csfb.com/primetrade/

index.shtml) by Credit Suisse First Boston, AutoBahn (www.autobahn.db.com) by Deutsche Bank, and Lehman Live (www.lehmanlive.com/) by Lehman Brothers.

■ *Consortiums.* In order to bring competitive prices and increased liquidity, and share in the burdensome technology costs of building and maintaining these platforms, some investment banks came together to form online trading platforms, while maintaining their own proprietary systems. This move also made it possible to compete with independent platforms, which are not able to enjoy the support of dealers to provide liquidity. Examples of such systems include TradeWeb (www.tradeweb.com) by Credit Suisse First Boston, Goldman Sachs, Lehman Brothers, Merrill Lynch, Morgan Stanley Dean Witter, Salomon Smith Barney, Deutsche Bank, Barclays Capital, JP Morgan Chase, Greenwich Capital, ABN AMRO, Bear Stearns, and UBS Warburg; BondClick (www.bondclick.com) by ABN AMRO, Barclays Capital, BNP Paribas, Caboto, Deutsche Bank, Dresdner Bank, and JP Morgan Chase; and Asiabondportal (www.asiabondportal.com) by ABN AMRO, Daiwa SBCM, Deutsche Bank, Income Partners, JP Morgan Chase, and UBS Warburg. Beyond joint liquidity support, large dealers have also joined together to roll out joint content sites such as BondHub (www.bondhub.com), which gives users access to all joint fixed-income and other research produced by a group of the largest U.S. dealers.

■ *Independent systems.* Online trading systems independent of dealers have had little success. Without the support of a dealer, these systems usually fail to meet investors liquidity and content needs. However, some systems that specialize in specific securities and markets have been able to survive. Better-known examples are Currenex, Blackbird, and Apogean Technology.

Sources of prices for securities

■ *Single-dealer systems.* These systems allow investors to execute transactions with a single dealer. These are less preferable to investors due to limited price competition and usually serve the existing customer base. But most single-dealer systems are able to offer trading in multiple products, so some institutional investors trading in more than one type of product still prefer these sites. Examples include Autobahn and WebET.

■ *Multidealer systems.* These systems allow traders to get prices from and trade with multiple dealers, increasing liquidity and price competition. Examples include MarketAxess and TradeWeb.

Customer base

■ *Dealer-to-dealer (interdealer) systems.* Only dealers can access these systems. The multilateral interaction in an interdealer system allows dealers to get competitive prices for their positions and trade anonymously. Trading in foreign exchange and derivatives markets tends to take place on interdealer electronic platforms. Examples are Reuters Dealing 2000-2, EuroMTS, and eSpeed.

■ *Dealer-to-customer systems.* These systems allow online trading between dealers and institutional investors. Examples are TradeWeb, MarketAxess, and BondClick. Some interdealer systems, such as eSpeed, are getting ready to open their services to institutional investors.

Coverage and products

Online trading systems vary in terms of the products they cover and the markets in which they operate. Some multidealer trading systems specialize in one kind of security in one market (such as the United States), while some trading systems allow electronic trading of multiple securities in many markets.

- eSpeed allows electronic trading of multiple types of securities (munis, treasury securities, repos) in G-10 countries and emerging markets. Asiabondportal is a consortium-owned trading platform that allows institutional investors to trade in Asian bonds. MuniAuction is a dealer-to-customer auction trading platform for municipal securities and money market instruments.
- Trading in interdealer foreign exchange markets is dominated by electronic trading systems. Reuters Dealing 2000-1 and 2000-2, EBS, Currenex, and FX Connect are systems specializing in foreign exchange and foreign exchange derivatives trading.
- In June 2000 Apogean Technology and IBM launched a business-to-business e-marketplace for trading emerging markets debt, including Brady bonds. POEMS (Phillips Online Electronic Mart System) and patagon.com are systems for e-trading stocks and fixed-income securities in Asia and Latin America.

Table A3-1 provides an overview of some fixed-income trading systems.

E-trading in equity markets

Online trading in global equity markets was led by the introduction of continental European electronic exchanges and electronic communication networks that used efficient technologies to lower transaction costs and geographic limitations in stock trading. This has created many opportunities for global financial markets as well as challenges in regulating and managing these opportunities.

The trading models in equity markets can be divided into two categories. Order-driven systems combine all bid and ask orders into one central order book and automatically match the orders without any intermediaries. The major automated stock exchanges use these systems to automatically match the orders of dealers. Quote-driven systems bring together dealers that provide two-way prices for securities. The bid-ask spread generates the profit for these systems.

Electronic communication networks

Using a computerized network, investors can place their bid price for a share of stock or set their own selling price in an of f-exchange market. These systems are known as electronic communication networks (ECNs). The biggest users of ECNs are institutional investors, such as mutual fund and pension fund managers, who are not members of stock exchanges. ECNs connect buyers and sellers on en electronic network without relying on brokers, so trading is cheaper and quicker. Examples of ECNs are Instinet (owned by Reuters), Archipelago, Island, and Europe s Tradepoint.

Table A3-1

Fixed-income trading systems

Auction systems

System	Ownership	Owner	Price source	Customer-base	Product	Coverage
MuniAuction	Investment bank	Grant Street Securities	Single-dealer	Dealer-to-customer	Municipal securities, money market instruments	U.S.
EBondUSA.com	Independent	Privately-held	Multi-dealer	Dealer-to-customer	Agency, asset-backed corporate, mortgage-backed, and Treasury securities	U.S.
Bloomberg Secondary Market Auction System	Independent	Bloomberg	Multi-dealer	Dealer-to-customer	Federal agency, corporate, mortgage-backed, and asset-backed securities	U.S.
Valubond	Independent	FTVentures, Alliance. Technology Ventures, J.P. Morgan Chase, Zions Bancorporation and Wasatch Ventures	Multi-dealer	Dealer-to-customer	Agency, corporate, municipal, and Treasury securities	U.S.

Inquiry-based systems

System	Ownership	Owner	Price source	Customer-base	Product	Coverage
TradeWeb	Consortium	CSFB, Goldman Sachs, Lehman Brothers, Merrill Lynch, MSDW, SSB, Deutsche Bank, Barclays, JP Morgan Chase, Greenwich Capital, ABN AMRO, Bear Stearns, UBS Warburg	Multi-dealer	Dealer-to-customer	U.S. Treasury, agency, Euro Sovereigns, and TBA-MBS securities	U.S.
MarketAxess	Consortium	ABN AMRO, JP Morgan Chase, Deutsche Bank, Chase Manhattan, UBS Warburg, Bear Stearns, Lehman Brothers Holdings, Credit Suisse First Boston	Multi-dealer	Dealer-to-customer	Agency, corporate, European, municipal, and Treasury securities	U.S.
BondClick	Consortium	ABN AMRO, Barclays, BNP Paribas, Caboto, Deutsche Bank, Dresdner Bank, JP Morgan Chase	Multi-dealer	Dealer-to-customer	Euro government bonds	Europe
PrimeTrade	Investment bank	Credit Suisse First Boston	Single-dealer	Dealer-to-customer	Derivatives, foreign exchange, government and credit bonds	U.S., Asia
Bloomberg	Independent	Bloomberg dealer	Multi-customer	Dealer-to-	Treasury securities	U.S.

Table A3-1

Fixed-income trading systems (continued)

Cross-matching systems

System	Ownership	Owners	Price source	Customer-base	Product	Coverage
BondBook	Consortium	Goldman Sachs, Merrill Lynch, MSDW	Multi-dealer	Dealer-to-dealer	Investment grade and high-yield corporate and municipal bonds	U.S.
BondDesk	Consortium	ABN AMRO, Bank of America, BondExchange LLC, Bear Stearns First Union	Multi-dealer	Dealer-to-customer	Agency, corporate, municipal, and Treasury securities	U.S.
BondsinAsia	Consortium	BRIDGE eMarkets, Citigroup, Deutsche Bank, HSBC	Multi-dealer	Dealer-to-dealer	Domestic government and corporate bonds	Asia (regional franchises)
Broker Tec	Consortium	ABN AMRO, Banco Capital, CSFB, Deutsche Bank, Dresdner Bank, Goldman Sachs, Lehman Brothers, Merrill Lynch, MSDW, SSB, UBS Warburg	Multi-Santander, Barclays	Dealer-to-dealer	Agency and Treasury securities	U.S., Europe dealer
EuroMTS	Consortium	More than 20 dealers	Multi-dealer	Dealer-to-dealer	Government bonds, eurobonds	Europe
eSpeed	Investment bank	Cantor Fitzgerald Securities	Multi-dealer	Dealer-to-dealer	Government bonds, Eurobonds, corporate bonds, U.K. gilts, emerging market securities, repos, and municipal securities	U.S., G-7, Europe, emerging markets
Autobahn	Investment	Deutsche Bank	Single-dealer	Dealer-to-customer	U.S. Treasury and agency securities, European government and semi-government bonds	U.S., Europe
Apogean Technologies	Independent	Apogean Capital	Multi-dealer	Dealer-to-dealer	Emerging market debt securities	Emerging markets
Currenex	Independent	Venture capitalists	Multi-dealer	Dealer-to-dealer	Foreign exchange	U.S., Europe
Instinet	Independent	Amerindo, Barclays Capital, TH Lee.Putnam Internet Partners, Dutch/Shell, WR Hambrecht & Co	Multi-dealer	Dealer-to-dealer	Treasury securities, euro sovereigns	U.S., Europe

Note: Online trading systems that use cross-matching vary in the level of access they provide. At one extreme are open architecture systems that allow access to all kinds of traders, where an infinite number of clients can trade anonymously. At the other extreme are interdealer systems that give access only to dealers to trade on their site so, although the participants trade with each other anonymously, the number of traders is limited to the number of allowed users.

Source: Claessens, Glaessner, Klingebiel, 2001.

Online stock brokerages

Online discount brokerages offer order routing services to their subscribers for a flat fee for each transaction. Due to the high competition in the industry, these fees can be as low as $6 a transaction. In Korea, where commissions on online trades are at an all-time low due to high trading volume and low fees, some online brokerages are incurring losses or even closing their doors. These online stock brokerages provide their customers with low-cost or free research and analysis on stocks. Most online brokerages give their customers the ability to make bids for initial public offerings (IPOs) and provide banking facilities, treating the accounts like regular bank checking accounts. Most online stock trading in emerging markets occurs through Internet brokerages that redirect orders to the major exchanges. In some of these countries alternative trading systems (ATSs), which are ECNs that function as exchanges, are allowed on a limited basis in order to avoid dilution of liquidity from exchanges in relatively small markets. Some big players in the U.S. market are listed in Table A3-2.

Table A3-2
Major U.S. online stock brokerages

Brokerage	Commission (market/limit order)	Online banking	Checking accounts	Option trading	Phone helpline	Bonds via phone	Mutual funds
			Features				
Charles Schwab & Co.	$29.95		●		●		●
Fidelity	$25.00		●		●		●
Merrill Lynch & Competitiveness	$29.95		●	●	●	●	●
TD Waterhouse Inc.	$12.00		●	●	●	●	●
E*Trade	$14.75/$19.95	●	●	●	●	●	●
Ameritrade	$8.00/$13.00		●	●	●	●	●
DLJ Direct	$20.00		●	●	●	●	●
Datek Online	$9.99				●		●
National Discount Brokers	$14.75/$19.75		●	●	●	●	●

Source: Basics of Stock Trading Online, http://onlinebrokerage.about.com/money/onlinebrokerage/cs/webtradingbasics/

Most of these brokerages are expanding their services globally and forming joint ventures with local brokerages in emerging markets. An example is SE Global Equities Company Limited (SEG), a subsidiary of Capital Alliance Group that has expanded its network of global trading alliances with more than 100 brokerages covering 50 stock exchanges around the world.

Direct access trading

Direct access trading is online trading where, when an investor makes an order online, the brokerage firm routes the order directly to a market maker and gets a commission from the market maker called a payment for order flow. Direct access usually routes the trade to an electronic clearing network or a small order execution system.

Investors have to download special software to trade in this environment. This is a more complicated trading environment than the other online brokerages, so investors tend to be more sophisticated institutional investors or day traders. Examples of direct access brokerages include the following.

Brokerage	Cost per 500 trades a month
CyberTrader	$9.95
SourceTrade	$16.00
EdgeTrade	$8.95
Firefly Platinum Pro	$9.95
Trade WallStreet	$9.95

Source: Claessens, Glaessner, Klingebiel, 2001.

Emerging markets

Examples of online stock trading initiatives in emerging markets include the following.

Eastern Europe

■ Electronic System for Trading Securities on the Stock Exchange and OTC Market (Albania, Bosnia and Herzegovina, Bulgaria, Croatia, Macedonia, Romania). Economic Construction and Development in Southeast Europe a joint World Bank-European Commission Website that aims to coordinate assistance to countries in the region has posted a proposal to establish an electronic system for trading securities on the stock exchange and over the counter market. The project aims to establish an integrated, efficient, and transparent capital market, raise investment activity in these countries, legitimize and popularize trade companies, and attract foreign investments to the region. (www.seerecon.org/NewIdeas/BIA/4.htm)

■ Sati Online Brokerage, the first broker in the Czech Republic, has developed a system of Internet-based stock handling that is used by clients from the Czech Republic and abroad.

■ Hungary has only a few brokerage firms using the Internet for online trading on the Budapest Stock Exchange. These firms include Quaestor Financial Group, Equitas, and Internet Broker Kft.

Asia

■ Karachi Stock.com (Pakistan) offers its members and visitors online and offline stock trading on the Karachi Stock Exchange and processes orders to buy or sell stocks on the exchange.

■ DFNN.com is a Philippine-based application services provider, financial e-commerce solutions provider, financial portal, and online stock trading firm. The portal provides free access to updated stock quotes, research reports, technical analysis, news headlines, market commentary, and product information on various financial products and services, all of which helps users decide what financial transaction to make (online trading, online banking, and so on).

■ Phillips Online Electronic Mart System, a Singapore-based nonbank online broker, offers online trading on three regional exchanges Hong Kong (China), Kuala Lumpur (Malaysia), and Singapore.

■ Asian Capital Equities, a Philippines-based online stock broker, is a joint venture between the Hong Kong (China)-based Bank of East Asia, the Philippine investment banking pioneer East Asia Capital Corporation, the Malaysian conglomerate affiliate MUI Philippines, and individual Filipino investors. Incorporated in 1989, the company was the first Philippine brokerage house to go online and now averages 1 billion Philippine pesos in annual transactions.

■ Korea Samsung Securities Cyber Stock offers trading, quotes, charts, and real-time trading for Korean securities.

■ ARKaccess Asia Limited a multibroker trading platform that will allow efficient and virtually direct access to local members of multiple Asian-Pacific securities exchanges from anywhere in the world. The routing system, ARKlink, will be introduced in the second half of 2001 in five Asian markets Australia, Hong Kong (China), Japan, Singapore, and Thailand as well as the United Kingdom and the United States. ARKmatch, the matching system, will be introduced later.

Latin America

■ Patagon.com is a Latin American online brokerage for stock trading and personal financial management.

■ Rava Sociedad de Bolsa is Argentina s online stock trading firm.

■ Hedging Griffo is Brazil s online stock trading firm.

Annex 4: Selected Smart Card Projects in Emerging Markets and Developing Countries

Africa	Card	Institution	Project description
Common Market for Eastern and Southern Africa (COMESA)	**Mondex e-cash:** multifunctional purse divided into five pockets allowing up to five currencies to be held at a time. Can also be used across open networks such as telephony or the Internet	Eastern and Southern African Trade and Development Bank (PTA Bank)	The Eastern and Southern African Trade and Development Bank (PTA Bank) purchased the franchise rights for Mondex, The deal, which is on behalf of the Committee of COMESA Central Bank Governors, may be the largest government endorsement of smart card technology and follows on the five existing Mondex franchises in Africa (Ghana, Lesotho, Namibia, South Africa, and Swaziland). Mondex e-cash application allows for offline transactions and has multicurrency and cross-border capability. Because it allows for the transfer of value between cards without the need to centrally record every transaction, the application can function without developing a costly and comprehensive traditional infrastructure to support it. Mondex also offers the ability to download value directly from chip to chip using a phone, bringing flexibility to retailers and consumers at relatively low cost. Mondex's unique security architecture allows for person to person transfer of e-cash and enables cardholders to carry up to five currencies at once. This interoperability means that Mondex's technology is flexible enough to be used as an alternative to cash across a number of COMESA territories.
http://www.mondex.ca/eng/media/pr23.htm			
Ghana	**Visa Horizon:** chip-based, pre-authorized offline payment card	Visa International, Standard Chartered Bank Ghana	Visa International and Standard Chartered Bank Ghana launched the first domestic Visa card in a West African country and the first public use of Visa Horizon, a chip-based, preauthorized offline payment card. The program marks the first large-scale rollout of Visa Horizon, with up to 100,000 offline domestic debit cards being issued and over 300 merchant signups over the next five years. It is also the largest planned implementation of chip payment technology in West Africa and an example of how chip cards can be used to overcome telecommunications weaknesses in new markets.
www.visa.com/av/news/press_release.ghtml?pr_form_edit=330&edit_file=			
Ghana	**Mondex e-cash:** multifunctional purse divided into five pockets allowing up to five currencies to be held at a time. Can also be used across open networks such as telephony or the Internet	Mondex Ghana Ltd.	Hitachi Europe won a contract to supply a smart card–based, electronic banking solution to Mondex Ghana Ltd., a joint venture company established by Ghana's two leading financial institutions—Ghana Commercial Bank and Agricultural Development Bank—to exploit the Mondex e-cash franchise. Mondex Ghana intends to deploy the innovative Mondex e-cash system in phases to bring modern banking to over 18 million Ghanaians (90 percent of whom do not have bank services). The project, worth in excess of $2 million, is the first example of an e-cash banking project in West Africa.
http://www.hitachi-eu.com/smartcommerce/news/ghana.html			
Nigeria	**E-purse card**	Securecard Trust Group	Securecard Trust Co. Ltd., which licenses the Proton technology in Nigeria, plans to have 100,000 mainly electronic purse cards in the market by the end of 2000 and 500,000 cards by the end of 2003. The Nigerian banks that make up the Securecard Trust Group plan to convert an existing 15,000-card e-purse project, Diamond Bank Paycard, to Proton. In addition, the banks will use Proton for salary payment and club membership cards they plan to issue.
www.cardtech.faulknergray.com/arch00.htm			

Africa	Card	Institution	Project description
South Africa	**Visa Cash:** card loaded or with predefined value designed for secure payments over the Internet and mobile phones, and for low-value purchases	Visa International, South Africa's PEP Bank	South Africa's PEP Bank will be the first issuer of Visa Cash stored-value chip cards using Proton technology. In a one-year pilot launched in November 2000, the bank will issue 10,000 chip cards to its customers and another 15,000 cards to individuals without bank accounts. Users will be able to load money onto the cards at terminals in railways stations, banks, shops, and other public areas in the Cape Town area. The cards will have a $74 limit. Two stations of the commuter rail operator Metrorail will accept Proton for payment, and Visa International and Proton World executives say the pilot is their first step into the mass transit sector in a country where most adults lack bank accounts but often ride buses and trains.
www.cardtech.faulknergray.com/arch00.htm			
South Africa	**Mondex e-cash:** multifunctional purse divided into five pockets allowing up to five currencies to be held at a time. Can also be used across open networks such as telephony or the Internet	Mondex International	U.K.-based smart card firm Mondex International has designed an electronic cash and banking system to be adopted and incorporated through the South African Post Office's 2,000 Post Bank counters. This smart card project will enable people to set up pseudo bank accounts, with biometrics technology using fingerprints to provide reliable identification. The e-bank accounts can be used in a variety of ways. When a cardholder has paid in benefits or wages, he or she can transfer direct payments to organizations such as the church (in most regions community members pay a regular subscription to the church). Alternatively, they can set up savings pools in which they store money they are saving to pay for something specific, such as education. Although all the money is held on the same smart card, the different pools enable people to take a more planned approach to their finances, and the direct payment facility provides guaranteed transfer of funds without inappropriate and costly intervention.
http://www.jrc.es/cfapp/leodb/kw.cfm?kword=241			

Asia	Card	Institution	Project description
China	**Chip-based cards:** multifunctional debit and credit smart cards	Major banks in China	Several major banks in China have launched pilots of chip-based debit cards in Beijing and Changsha using standardized card and point-of-sale terminal software adopted by China's central bank, the People's Bank of China. The pilots could lead to the large-scale rollout of interoperable debit and credit smart cards nationwide as one of China's Golden Card projects. The pilots will last about two years. Many of the same banks, among them the state-run Bank of China, Industrial and Commercial Bank of China, and Construction Bank of China, launched a similar test of several thousand standardized cards in Shanghai in December 2000.
www.cardtech.faulknergray.com/arch00.htm			
Hong Kong, China	**i.Life card:** multifunctional credit, debit, and other	Hongkong and Shanghai Banking Corporation Limited	Hong Kong's major full-service communications provider, Cable & Wireless HKT, and the Hongkong and Shanghai Banking Corporation Limited (HSBC) jointly launched i.Life Card, a high-capacity smart card that will bring enhanced security and convenience to online shopping and electronic transactions. The multifunctional card is the first of its kind in the market and was developed to meet the growing need for sophisticated e-commerce applications. Credit and debit card functions, international calling, Mondex e-cash, and chip-based e-commerce applications have been combined on a single card. i.Life Card is also the first in Hong Kong to provide a carrier for electronic certificates such as Hongkong Post's e-Cert. The electronic certificate carrier facilitates e-commerce and online transactions that require identity authentication. It als demonstrates the card's vast ability to support innovative e-applications.
http://www.multos.com/multos_cd2/Marketing/PressReleases/00-06-22.HSBC.iLife%20Card.Launch.PDF			
India	**E-purse and EMV-compliant debit:** e-purse targeted at micropayments and the debit application at higher-value day-to-day transactions	ALW	In July 2000 Proton World and Alittleworld.com Private Limited (ALW) signed agreements granting ALW Proton operating licenses for India and the Philippines. ALW is an Indian technology company with a mission to "redefine the future of money" in developing countries. ALW will provide technology integration, operational support, and a mass deployment implementation model for issuers such as banks, post offices, and telecom companies. It will initially offer smart cards in both countries with either or both of two Proton applications, the electronic purse and Europay, MasterCard, Visa (EMV) compliant debit. The e-purse will be targeted at micropayments and the debit application at higher-value day-to-day transactions, with both offering full auditability and the world-renowned Proton end-to-end security. ALW's Proton-based dual-purpose smart cards will provide users with a secure and practical alternative to cash without the limitations on eligibility or restrictions on use associated with credit cards in developing countries.
www.protonworld.com/press/releases/press63index.htm			

Asia	Card	Institution	Project description
Indonesia	**Paspor BCA/Maestro/ Cirrus card:** PIN-based, online, real-time debit program	MasterCard, BCA	MasterCard International and BCA—the biggest private bank in Indonesia, with 800 online branches and 8 million customers—introduced the Paspor BCA/Maestro/ Cirrus card, allowing millions of Paspor BCA cardholders to access Maestro and Cirrus facilities. Maestro, MasterCard's global debit brand, is the region's only personal identification number or PIN-based, online, real-time debit program. The MasterCard Cirrus/Maestro network allows cardholders to withdraw local currency from their accounts at over 560,000 Cirrus ATMs in 102 countries.
	www.mastercard.com/about/press/pressreleases.cgi?id=344		
Korea, Rep. of	**Mondex e-cash and MasterCard M/Chip:** multifunctional—credit, debit, and other	MasterCard Korea, Kookmin Credit Card	One of Korea's largest credit card companies, Kookmin Credit Card, and MasterCard Korea are to jointly introduce one of the first multifunctional smart cards, with both chip and e-cash functionality. The card, called the Kookmin Trade Pass Card, will integrate multiple applications such as credit card, debit, electronic wallet, identification card, and automated passenger clearance. Operating on the Multos smart card platform, the cards will have credit and debit functionality through MasterCard's credit and debit application, M/Chip. Cash purchases will be enabled by Mondex's e-cash application. Cardholders will be able to choose either program for specific financial transactions.
	www.epaynews.com/archives/index.cgi?ref=browse&f=view&id=98225113121212015050		
Korea, Rep. of	**Multiapplication card:** with an electronic purse and credit application	Pusan Bank of South Korea	In July 2000 Pusan Bank of South Korea announced that it will issue 1 million multiapplication smart cards, letting Pusan cardholders pay fares on trains and buses, make purchases at stores and vending machines, and even pay taxes over the Internet. According to KEB Technology Co., the Korean systems integrator on the project, the cards will include an electronic purse and credit application from the bank, which cardholders will be able to use at 10,000 point-of-sale terminals in 2000 and another 10,000 in 2001. Cardholders will also be able to recharge the transit and bank e-purses over the Internet at computer kiosks or on their home computers, as well as at 1,100 reloading machines and ATMs.
	www.cardtech.faulknergray.com/arch00.htm		
Korea, Rep. of	**Visa Cash:** card loaded or with predefined value designed for secure payments over the Internet and mobile phones, and for low-value purchases	Visa International, various Korean institutions	In June 2000 Visa International announced that it would lead a group in Korea that includes 13 financial institutions and mobile phone operator SK Telecom to issue 10 million e-purse cards over the next five years for making purchases over the Internet and at physical retail shops. The system will use the Network for Electronic Transfers (NETS), a Singaporean company that processes more than 100 million card transactions a year.
	www.cardtech.faulknergray.com/arch00.htm		

Asia	Card	Institution	Project description
Philippines	**Visa Cash:** card loaded or with predefined value designed for secure payments over the Internet and mobile phones, and for low-value purchases	Visa International, major banks in the Philippines	Visa International has announced that several banks in the Philippines intend to roll out 10 million Visa Cash electronic purse cards by 2005. The banks, among them Equitable Bank, Metro Bank, Union Bank, Banco De Oro, and First E-Bank, signed a memo of understanding with several other partners, including the Philippines Long Distance Telephone Co., the country's largest telecommunications company; 7-Eleven stores and other retailers; and two major theme parks. The partners will accept the reloadable cards, which will also be used on the Internet. The phone company now issues more than 14 million of its own chip-based prepaid phone cards each year.
www.cardtech.faulknergray.com/arch00.htm			
Philippines	**Mondex e-cash:** multifunctional purse divided into five pockets allowing up to five currencies to be held at a time. Can also be used across open networks such as telephony or the Internet	Mondex Philippines Inc.	In October 2000 Mondex Philippines projected a cardholder base of at least 800,000, with 500 Mondex loading stations and at least 15,000 commercial establishments in different industries. Mondex e-cash gives issuers greater flexibility and control over the range of services they can provide, and can be used across open networks such as telephony or the Internet. It is ideal for high-volume, low-value payments. Under an agreement with MasterCard International and Mondex Asia, Mondex Philippines has the license to operate Mondex technology for the local market. The company also has the right to promote and license the technology to financial institutions, merchant establishments, and other service providers in its nationwide deployment of Mondex chip-based cards.
http://www.mondexphil.com/press/press_CARDrollout.html			
Singapore	**Cash withdrawal**	Network for Electronic Transfers (Singapore), local banks	In March 2001 the Network for Electronic Transfers (NETS) launched a service that enables Singaporeans to withdraw funds from their bank accounts at retail outlets using ATM cards. This is part of a move to improve accessibility to cash withdrawal facilities. The CashBack service is available to ATM cardholders of DBS Bank, Keppel TatLee Bank, OCBC Bank, Overseas Union Bank, and United Overseas Bank. The service operates as part of NETS's Electronic Funds Transfer at Point of Sale (EFTPOS) service, a direct payment facility that allows retailers to debit a customer's bank account at the time of purchase. Consumers are able to withdraw funds with or without making a purchase, depending on the retailer. The amount that can be withdrawn will depend on the availability of cash held in the store. Like all EFTPOS payments, NETS does not impose a charge on the consumer.
www.nets.com.sg/news/article.php?artID=11			

Asia	Card	Institution	Project description
Singapore	**CashCard TopUp over the Internet**: uses E-Wallet, a software application that enables the CashCard to be credited and debited over the Internet	Network for Electronic Transfers (Singapore), local banks	In August 2000 the Network for Electronic Transfers (NETS) introduced a feature that will enable users o top up their telectronic purses over the Internet. CashCard TopUp over the Internet will provide users with more access points and greater ease. On launching the application, users will be guided through a series of instructions that include entering the top-up amount and a HomeNETS Personal Identification Number (PIN). The HomeNETS PIN is used solely for CashCard top-ups on HomeNETS terminals, mobile phones, and the Internet. With the CashCard inserted in the smart card reader, E-Wallet will credit the CashCard with the amount to be topped up upon receiving approval from the user's bank. CashCards can be topped up using ATMs, NETS kiosks, HomeNETS terminals, and mobile phones, and at major gasoline stations.
www.nets.com.sg/news/article.php?artID=9			
Singapore	**CashCard TopUp on mobile phones**: uses a dual-slot mobile phone, a smart ATM card, and a HomeNETS PIN	Network for Electronic Transfers (Singapore), local banks	In April 2000 MobileOne (M1) and the Network for Electronic Transfers (NETS) announced that CashCards, widely used by motorists and other consumers in Singapore, can now be topped up over mobile phones. All users require is a dual-slot mobile phone, a smart ATM card, and a HomeNETS PIN. The smart ATM card and HomeNETS PIN can be obtained from the user's bank. Customers can also use the service to check the balance on their CashCards and to view previous card transactions. Future applications include a service that will enable M1 customers to pay bills using their mobile phones.
www.nets.com.sg/news/article.php?artID=5			
Thailand	**Visa Cash**: card loaded or with predefined value designed for secure payments over the Internet and mobile phones, and for low-value purchases	Visa International, various Thai banks	The Thai Smart Card Consortium—formed by 7-Eleven, Bank, Siam Commercial Bank, and Bangkok Bank—has Visa Cash, Visa's e-purse, as the payment brand for the consortium's electronic purse project. Visa Cash uses chip card technology and is designed for use for secure payments over the Internet and mobile phones and for low-value purchases such as those made in fast food restaurants, convenience stores, vending machines, payphones, or gasoline stations. Visa Cash facilitates fast and convenient transactions without the need for signature or PIN. The introduction of Visa Cash will stimulate the use of electronic cash in Thailand and move the economy one step closer to a cashless society.
www.businessinthailandmag.com/archive/jul00/29.html			

Europe	Card	Institution	Project description
Baltic states (Estonia, Latvia, Lithuania)	**Smart card retail loyalty schemes**	Unibanka	In January 2001, Proton World and Netcard announced that Netcard has become the Proton licensee in Estonia, Latvia, and Lithuania. Netcard is a smart card company based in Riga, Latvia, that has developed two smart card retail loyalty schemes. In 1999, in association with information technology provider BISS and Unibanka (Latvia's largest bank), Netcard developed an access control system for cars in the Old Town district of Riga, where over 5,000 cards have been issued out of a planned total of 20,000.
www.protonworld.com/press/releases/2001/press_2001_01_03_index.htm			
Bulgaria	**Proton e-purse:** with Proton R3 and R4 technologies and CEPS and EMV	BORICA	In December 2000 Proton World and BORICA signed a binding agreement under which BORICA, the operator of Bulgaria's payment card network, became the Proton licensee for Bulgaria. BORICA processes domestic and international payment card transactions for 25 Bulgarian banks and supports the ATM and point-of-sale terminal network. BORICA's smart card program will begin by the end of 2001 with three pilots managed by Proton World. The first will be the development of a domestic electronic purse smart card using well-established Proton R3 technology. The second will use Proton World's new R4 technology to provide secure access, digital signatures, and secure e-commerce and mobile-commerce. The third pilot will be a field test of the R4 e-purse, interoperable CEPS-based [Common Electronic Purse Specification] e-purse, and EMV credit and debit applications, which will precede the migration of Bulgaria's 550,000 magnetic-stripe payment cards to R4 smart cards.
www.protonworld.com/press/releases/press76index.htm			
Croatia	**MBU smart cards** with the Proton e-purse and chip-based credit and debit applications	Consortium of 27 local banks	In January 2000 MBU, a consortium of 27 banks in Croatia, licensed the Proton electronic purse system for smart cards. Proton World will manage a two-stage project for MBU, whose members have issued 500,000 debit cards. In the first phase, to begin in February 2001, MBU will replace its point-of-sale terminals with C-Zam/Smash POS terminals that accept smart cards from Belgium's Banksys bank association, a part owner of Proton World. In the second phase MBU members will replace their magnetic-stripe cards with smart cards carrying the Proton e-purse and chip-based credit and debit applications.
www.cardtech.faulknergray.com/arch00.htm			
Turkey	**Multifunctional credit, debit, and other**	Garanti Bank	In July 2000 it was announced that Turkey's Garanti Bank will issue 750,000 smart cards with credit, debit, and loyalty features. U.S.-based Hypercom is supplying 2,500 point-of-sale terminals to merchants participating in the program. The terminals have touch-screens that allow consumers to view their accumulated loyalty points and to use the points for discounts on purchases. The bank's card will carry a MasterCard logo and will comply with the EMV standards for chip-based credit and debit applications developed by Europay International, MasterCard International, and Visa International.
www.cardtech.faulknergray.com/arch00.htm			

Latin America	Card	Institution	Project description
Brazil	**MasterCard M/Chip**: multifunctional credit, debit, and other	MasterCard, major banks in Brazil	At least 240,000 of the 16 million MasterCard cardholders in Brazil will take part in MasterCard's pioneering project occurring throughout Latin America. In partnership with its member financial institutions in Brazil—Bradesco, Caixa, Credicard, Itaœ, Real ABN AMRO, Unibanco and Redecard—MasterCard is initiating the migration from magnetic-stripe to smart cards. It expects that by the mid-2000s all the company's credit cards will be operating on the new platform. This effort will provide an infrastructure for combining several applications on a single card—including credit, debit, loyalty programs, and others—to create a powerful tool for launching and developing new products and services.
www.mastercard.com/about/press/pressreleases.cgi?id=369			
Latin America and the Caribbean	**Visa Cash**: card loaded or with predefined value designed for secure payments over the Internet and mobile phones, and for low-value purchases	Visa LAC Region	Proton World has signed an agreement with Visa International Latin America and Caribbean Region for the joint marketing of Proton-based e-purse smart card systems that are compatible with Visa Cash in most of the region. The Proton technology allows dynamic creation of applications, conforms to EMV specifications, will conform to CEPS and Global Platform, is open to multiple sourcing of chips, cards, and terminals from certified manufacturers, and can be integrated with a contact or contactless system. The technology is also used in diverse applications such as telecommunications, access control, cardholder identification, closed user groups, automated transport fare collection, and secure Internet payments. It is compatible with all of the world's leading smart card platforms.
www.protonworld.com/press/releases/press47index.htm			
Mexico	**Proton e-purse**: multifunctional	Grupo Carso	A Mexican banking and telecommunications conglomerate plans to issue 6 million smart cards in 2001. The cards can be used and reloaded at 350,000 pay phones. The cards will carry the Proton electronic purse and merchant loyalty programs. The bank is part of Grupo Carso, which also owns Mexico's major phone company, Telefonas de Mexico (TelMex), and retail stores. The bank plans to expand its ATM base from 300 machines to 2,000, and to deploy 20,000 public kiosks where consumers will be able to reload the Proton cards. The cards will have chip-based credit and debit features that comply with international EMV standards.
www.ct-ctst.com/CT/			
Venezuela, RB	**Mondex e-cash**: multifunctional purse divided into five pockets allowing up to five currencies to be held at a time. Can also be used across open networks such as telephony or the Internet	Mondex Venezuela	In August 2000 ACI Worldwide announced that it has been chosen to provide Mondex system solutions to Mondex Venezuela and its members. Mondex Venezuela—a consortium formed by Banco Mercantil, Banco Universal, Banco Union, Consorcio Credicard, Banesco, and InterBank—will enable members, whether banks or nonbanks, to handle Mondex value and risk management services. The system will be able to handle Mondex smart card processing through traditional ATM and point-of-sale channels, as well as Mondex value transfer and customer service over the Internet.
http://www.aciworldwide.com/news/newsdetail.asp?news_id=145			

Annex 5: Selected E-Finance Examples in Emerging Markets and Developing Countries

Housing

Location	Project	Project summary
Hong Kong, China	Advantage Mortgage, specialized mortgage broker	Advantage Mortgage is a specialized mortgage broker in Hong Kong. The company derives its revenues from fees paid by 15 of the largest lenders in Hong Kong's real estate market as well as two lenders not supervised by the Hong Kong Monetary Authority. Advantage solicits borrowers, evaluates mortgage loan packages for presentation to borrowers through a kind of aggregator function, prepares all documentation required to underwrite the loan and ultimately send the loan package to final lenders, and provides offline support on documentation preparation by running a call center and interactive Web page dealing with such issues as the loan to value or debt service ratios required by lenders. Advantage is beginning to examine expansion to China, the Republic of Korea, and Taiwan (China).
www.advantagemortgage.com.hk/pda/index.htm		
Asia (various countries)	DollarDEX's online Reverse Auction and Group Mortgage	DollarDEX is a company that enables online consumers to compare, shop, auction, and apply for loans and insurance products from more than 30 leading financial institutions in Asia. In April 2000 it introduced the online Reverse Auction for housing loans, and in August 2000 the online Group Mortgage. The Reverse Auction gets banks to bid for groups of home mortgages from potential customers even before those customers have committed to the loans. DollarDEX.com's participating banks not only know more about what other banks are offering, but can also reduce their cost of customer acquisition. Some of these savings could be passed onto customers. The Group Mortgage allows borrowers to band together to get better deals from banks. In an arrangement with seven banks in Hong Kong, DollarDEX's new service—a first in South Asia—allow homeowners to present their loans collectively online for better packages from banks.
www.dollardex.com/		

Insurance

Location	Project	Project summary
China	Sohu.com and Taikang Online's consumer-oriented online insurance services	Sohu.com, a major web portal, and Taikang Online, a major insurer, have agreed to offer consumer-oriented insurance services online. Insurance consulting, services, and transactions will be provided to a variety of customers, including Internet users, insurance clients, insurance agents, and insurance companies. Taikang will use its e-commerce insurance platform to provide Sohu's registered users with online insurance services. Meanwhile, Sohu will share its information on registered users with Taikang to help expand its specialized online insurance market.
www.chinaonline.com/industry/financial/NewsArchive/Secure/2001/March/C01030606.asp		
Hong Kong, China	Re2R's online open exchange of insurance risk and reinsurance capacities	Re2Re is the first and only online marketplace providing open exchange of insurance risk and reinsurance capacities on a global basis. Re2Re uses proprietary Internet and e-commerce technology to dramatically improve reinsurance exchange among direct insurance companies, insurance brokers, reinsurance brokers, and reinsurance companies worldwide. Re2Re is a Bermuda-incorporated company with a regional office in Hong Kong and a service office in the Philippines.
www.re2re.com/		
Philippines	Yapster's online insurance service	Yapster.com is a cyber corporation that is hoping to become a contender in the local dot-com arena. It is owned by a Filipino-Chinese family engaged in various traditional businesses in the Philippines, including travel, mining, stocks and securities, textiles, manufacturing, and real estate. Part of the Yapster.com portal is 2insureAll, an online insurance service that provides benefits in case of losses to an insured individual. 2insureAll products include automobile, accident, fire, comprehensive general liability, electronic equipment, medical, life, and pre-need insurance.
www.yapster.com/ www.2insureall.com/		

Insurance (continued)

Location	Project	Project summary
Russian Federation	Renaissance Insurance Group, Russia's first e-insurance agency	Since November 1999 the Renaissance Insurance Group has been offering insurance services over the Internet. The main hindrance is the underdevelopment of card payments practice in the Russian Federation, but Renaissance Insurance has solved this problem by allowing customers who do not have a credit card to print the bill from the insurance site and pay it in the nearest bank office. In addition, the renins.com portal provides complete information on insurance markets, procedures, and terms. The virtual office is overseen by an online manager who can provide immediate help to customers.

agency.infoart.ru/it/news/engnews/99/12/06_584.htm
www.renins.com

| Turkey | The World Bank's Turkish Catastrophic Insurance Pool | The Turkish Catastrophic Insurance Pool is an Internet platform created by the Turkish government that allows customers to enter all personal information, including policy number and premium. Policies are issued on the Internet and the pool is monitored in real time. Since the pool's creation, 100,000 policies have been issued on the Web. |

| Asia (various countries) | DollarDEX Customized Travel Insurance | DollarDEX enables online consumers to compare, shop, auction, and apply for loans and insurance products from more than 30 leading financial institutions. Its Customized Travel Insurance lets insurance firms tailor travel insurance to consumers at flexible prices, and allows customers to request instant insurance quotations. |

www.dollardex.com/insurance/travel/index.cfm?show=travel_moreinfo.cfm

| Asia (various countries) | Asia's first fully online insurance product, from DollarDEX | DollarDEX recently pioneered the first fully online life insurance product, M@xivalue, which enables healthy applicants to get instant approval. DollarDEX's customers can get instant quotations based on a full comparison of features and prices, and can also buy online motor, travel, hospital, home, personal, long-term care, and even golfer's insurance. |

www.dollardex.com/press/index.cfm?show=i_insurance.htm

Microfinance

Location	Project	Project summary
Bangladesh	Grameen Bank and Grameen Phone's mobile phone project in rural Bangladesh	Grameen Bank, whose mission is to provide credit to the poorest of the rural poor, established Grameen Telecom to bring the information revolution to rural Bangladesh. Grameen Telecom provides two products. First, selected bank borrowers purchase pay phones (under the bank's lease program) and make them available to other villagers. Second, the Direct Subscriber program provides telephone service in rural areas that are not directly engaged in Grameen Bank activities. The phones have helped many poor women earn fair profits from their cow rearing, grocery stores, poultry farms, and vegetable gardening.

www.cisp.org/imp/december_99/12_99camp.htm
www.nation-online.com/200002/17/n0021706.htm#BODY8

Location	Project	Project summary
Nigeria	Smart cards for microcredit scheme	Gemcard Nigeria Limited has concluded plans to introduce smart cards targeted at the nonbanking segment of Nigerian society. The project is aimed at encouraging banking habits among the lower class as well as moving funds from the informal sector into the banking system. In addition, poor citizens will be given free smart cards and, with the active participation of banks in the smart pay scheme, a microcredit scheme will be created. Online banking services, available in a mobile van, will use a facial biometric system to recognize customers.

Source: Lagos Post Express, 23 November 2000.

Location	Project	Project summary
South Africa	Modified ATM services for the urban poor	In 1993 Standard Bank of South Africa created an affiliate, E Bank, to deliver basic banking services to the urban poor. E Bank provides financial services designed specifically for low-income clients, offering greater convenience for users while keeping under control the costs to the bank of providing services. E Bank combines the innovative technology of modified ATM services with staff available to help all clients. By rethinking the needs of basic bank customers, E Bank was able to bundle services valued by poorer clients to justify a fee high enough to cover costs.

Source: JoAnn Paulson, Financial Services for the Urban Poor, Policy Research Working Paper 2016, 1998, World Bank, Washington, D.C.

Location	Project	Project summary
Various countries	ACCIÓN's Palm Pilot project for microcredit lending	ACCIÓN International, one of the world's leading microfinance organizations, is using handheld computer technology (Palm Pilots) to cut the time and cost it takes to make a microloan. Loan officers typically record all data by hand because of the difficulty of carrying burdensome equipment when visiting clients. Recording data this way takes an average of 25 minutes per client. After the data is reentered at the office, total processing time stretches to an hour. New processing software, designed for Palm Pilots, allows loan officers to record client data, take applications, and make loan calculations on the spot. Back at the office, data can be quickly uploaded to a centralized database, eliminating the time-consuming task of entering it. Evaluating a client this way takes about 15 minutes. The new software was funded by the U.S. Agency for International Development.

www.accion.org/pdf/ventures_fall99.pdf
www.accion.org/press/main.asp

Location	Project	Project summary
Various countries	PlaNet Finance project using the Internet to refinance microfinance institutions	PlaNet Fund is the first international organization to refinance microfinance institutions. By using the Internet for worldwide coverage and maximum efficiency, PlaNet Fund aims to help microfinance institutions through all stages of their development. Its objective is to supply services such as loans, guarantees, joint funding, and bond purchases. In Bolivia, for example, a carpenter who needs new tools applies to a microfinance institution for a loan. The institution does not have sufficient funds at the time and so cannot provide the loan. But it can appeal over the Internet to PlaNet Fund, combining the applications of several craftsmen. A specialist on Bolivia and its institutions then examines the case. He gives his opinion to the operating committee of PlaNet Fund, which rapidly makes a decision—allowing the microfinance institution to meet its clients' needs.

www.planetfinance.org

Microfinance (continued)

Location	Project	Project summary
Various countries	UNCTAD's Virtual Microfinance Market	The Virtual Microfinance Market, developed by the United Nations Conference on Trade and Development (UNCTAD), is an information exchange system designed to facilitate interactions between microfinance institutions, private investors, governments, and other participants in the microfinance market. The system is aimed at creating sustainable market links between commercial investors worldwide and microenterprises in developing countries. It is expected to permit the investment, under commercial terms, of millions of dollars at the grassroots level and the creation of thousands of jobs. On its Internet site the Virtual Microfinance Market provides contact and financial information on microfinance institutions willing to mobilize commercial funding, information on the legal and regulatory conditions for investment in these institutions and links permitting direct contact with regulatory authorities in each country, contact data on investors and financial intermediaries and information on conditions attached to past or current offers, and access to sources of knowledge, technical advice, and training on state-of-the-art techniques and tools for improving microfinance institutions' financial management and access to capital markets.

www.vmm.dpn.ch/

Small and medium-size enterprises

Location	Project	Project description
Ghana	Computerized Mobile Bank	The Computerized Mobile Bank is an initiative of Ghana's Advanced Engineering Design and Research Corporation. It was funded by Infodev, a multidonor grant facility managed by the World Bank. The project designs, deploys, and operates a mobile bank to provide banking services to susu operators and small and medium-size enterprises in Ghana over 18 months. The objective is to determine the extent to which such a bank can expand the outreach of formal banking institutions and reduce the transaction costs of providing complete banking services to informal bankers (such as susu operators) and small and medium-size enterprises.

http://www.infodev.org/exchange/exch5.htm

Location	Project	Project description
Hong Kong, China	SMEloan	SMEloan is Hong Kong's leading provider of online financing to small and medium-size enterprises. The company has reengineered the commercial lending process by leveraging the power of the Internet. In addition, it manages and monitors credit risk using its proprietary Web-based risk management model. In October 2000 SMEloan achieved a first for a startup e-finance company in Asia by closing a HK$600 million financing facility with a group of banks led by Standard Chartered Bank and backed by a surety bond from Centre Solutions (Asia) Ltd.

www.gorillasia.com/tc/readarticle?id=1524

Location	Project	Project description
Various countries (Czech Republic, Hungary, India)	CitiBusiness	In April 1999 Citigroup created a new business group, CitiBusiness, that specializes in financial services for small and medium-size enterprises. In May 2000 the group launched CitiBusiness Platinum Select MasterCard, which in addition to providing generous lines of credit, gives access to various services—including the CitiBusiness Resource Network, which provides information on a range of subjects, from building a Website to setting up an employee benefits program. In early 2001 the group offered CitiBusiness Direct to small and medium-size enterprises in the Czech Republic, Hungary, and India. CitiBusiness Direct is a comprehensive Internet banking solution that previously was available only to large companies and multinational clients.

www.citibank.com
www.citibusinessdirect.com

Small and medium-size enterprises (continued)

Location	Project	Project Summary
Various countries	Tradehub Virtual MasterCard	In June 2000 MasterCard International signed a memorandum of understanding with an electronic trading activity center, Tradehub Asia.com, that builds and networks business-to-business multiproduct portals in Asia and the Pacific. MasterCard will act as the payment mechanism for all transactions undertaken through the TradeHub system, providing financial settlement across borders and currencies. The Tradehub Virtual MasterCard will be a catalyst for small and medium-size enterprises to trade with each other as well as major companies, both domestically and internationally.
www.mastercard.com/about/press/pressreleases.cgi?id=321		
Various countries	Virtual information and services network and smart cards for small and medium-size enterprises	Pride Africa, a financial institution that provides access to credit to over 80,000 entrepreneurs in Kenya, Malawi, Tanzania, Uganda, and Zambia, created Drumnet and Sunlink to overcome barriers to the growth of small and medium-size enterprises. DrumNet is a virtual information and services network linking clients to markets, information, and services. Through its network of microlending branches and information kiosks, Pride Africa's clients will have access to wholesale supplies and services, advertising, and partnership and association-building opportunities. To integrate microentrepreneurs with the formal financial sector, Pride Africa created Sunlink Cashpoints. Among others, Sunlink clients received smart cards that will serve as a client identification card helping to establish credit ratings, as a loan authorization card, and as a teller access card, facilitating access to formal financial services by small and medium-size enterprises.
www.prideafrica.com/		
Various countries	E-Finance Small Business, sponsored by the World Bank Group's International Finance Corporation	The E-Finance Small Business Initiative aims to help financial institutions increase the efficiency and volume of financial services targeted to small and medium-size enterprises by capitalizing on recent advancements in financial information and communication technologies. The goal is to create a model that will enable financial institutions to focus on the risk profiles and product needs of small and medium-size enterprises. To that end, the model will integrate technologies that allow financial institutions to collect and analyze significant amounts of client information on a real-time basis. The model is built around three factors that ensure sustained profitability in lending to small and medium-size enterprises: operating efficiency, asset quality, and growth. The pilot projects that are to put the e-finance model into practice will be launched in six regions. The International Finance Corporation's holistic approach to the initiative calls for several support activities, including a global credit bureau and a technology practice area for mobile banking and payment systems to facilitate noncash payment options for small and medium-size enterprises.
www.worldbank.org/html/fpd/privatesector/sme.htm www.ifc.org/sme/		

E-Finance Web Links

Annex 2: International E-finance working groups

Electronic Banking Group of the Basel Committee on Banking Supervision
The group issued *Fourteen Principles for Risk Management of Electronic Banking.* The full text of the report can be found at www.bis.org/publ.bcbs76.htm or www.bis.org

World Bank
The World Bank is reviewing the policy implications of changes in financial services, markets, and institutions driven by globalization and technological advances. http://www1.worldbank.org/finance

Financial Action Task Force (FATF)
The FATF is identifying the vulnerability of Internet banking to money laundering activities. www.oecd.org/fatf

International Organization of Securities Commissions (IOSC)
The Internet taskforce s report can be found at www.iosco.org/docs-public/1998-internet_security.html

International Association of Insurance Supervisors (IAIS)
The IAIS is reviewing developments in insurance activities on the Internet. www.iaisweb.org/framesets/about.html

Committee on the Global Financial System (CGFS)
The CGFS is assessing electronic trading in financial markets and studying its implications for financial stability. www.bis.org/cgfs/index.htm#pgtop

International Telecommunication Union (ITU)
The ITU serves as a forum to address policy issues related to e-commerce in developing countries. www.itu.int

United Nations Commission on International Trade Law (UNCITRAL)
The commission s study focused on transferable bills of lading in an electronic environment. www.uncitral.org/en-index.htm

Annex 3: Online trading systems

Trading platforms for fixed-income securities

Auction systems

- **MuniAuction:** conducts online auctions of municipal securities. www.grantstreet.com

- **EBondUSA.com:** provides price discovery and online trading services for investment grade municipal bonds. http://www.bondmarkets.com/research/ecommerce/eBONDUSA.shtml (Municipal bond trader eBondUSA is struggling to stay alive and is down to just five staffers as it waits for its trading technology to come online.)

- **Bloomberg Secondary Market Auction System:** www.bloomberg.com

- **Valubond:** a Web-based centralized marketplace for municipal, investment grade corporate, government, and federal agency debt. www.valubond.com

Inquiry-based systems

- **TradeWeb:** allows institutional customers to buy and sell U.S. Treasury and federal agency securities electronically with multiple primary dealers. www.tradeweb.com

- **Market Axess:** an Internet-based multidealer research and trading platform for credit products. www.marketaxess.com

- **BondClick:** a multidealer online trading platform designed for institutional investors. www.bondclick.com/ (BondVision and BondClick, the two Internet-based Dealer-to-Customer trading platforms for fixed income products have signed an agreement to merge their activities.)

- **PrimeTrade:** an Internet- and intranet-based real-time trading system of Credit Suisse First Boston. www.csfb.com/primetrade/index.shtml

- **Bloomberg BondTrader:** a multidealer electronic trading system for U.S. Treasury securities. www.bloomberg.com

Cross-matching systems

- **BondBook:** offers an online marketplace for investment grade and high-yield corporate and municipal bonds. www.bondbook.com

- **BondDesk:** a comprehensive trading platform for a wide array of fixed-income products. www.bonddesk.com/

- **BondsInAsia:** a regional electronic trading platform for Asian fixed-income securities. www.bondsinasia.com/

- **BrokerTec Global LLC:** a fully electronic interdealer broker active in U.S. and European capital markets. www.btec.com/

- **EuroMTS Limited:** a European e-trading system for euro-denominated benchmark government bonds. www.euromts-ltd.com/

- **eSpeed:** an interactive electronic marketplace that allows customers to execute transactions in a range of financial instruments. www.espeed.com

- **Autobahn:** launched by Deutsche Bank Securities, allows customers to conduct transactions electronically in U.S., European, and emerging market fixed-income securities, globally on a 24-hour basis. www.autobahn.db.com/

- **Apogean Technology:** an electronic trading system for dealers in emerging market debt securities. www.apogean.net

- **Currenex:** an independent, open financial exchange linking institutional foreign exchange buyers and sellers worldwide. www.currenex.com/

- **Instinet Fixed-income:** a global electronic broker service that facilitates trading in U.S. Treasury and Euro sovereign debt securities. www.instinet.com/

The Bond Market Association Survey offers a more comprehensive list of online trading platforms for fixed-income markets: www.bondmarkets.com/research/ecommerce/

Trading platforms for equity trading

Eastern Europe

- **Sati Online Brokerage** (Czech Republic): www.sati.cz/

- **Quaestor Financial Group** (Hungary): www.quaestor.hu/

- **Equitas** (Hungary): http://online.equitas.hu/

- **Internet Broker Kft** (Hungary): www.cd.hu/fw/vis/index.html

Asia

- **Karachistocks.com** (Pakistan): www.karachistocks.com

- **Phillips Online Electronic Mart System** (Singapore): www.poems.com.sg

- **Asian Capital Equities** (Phillipines, Malaysia, Thailand and Indonesia): https://www.psedirect.net

- **Korea Samsung Securities Cyber Stock:** http://english.samsungfn.com/

- **ARKaccess Asia Limited (Global):** www.arkaccess.com

Latin America

- **Patagon.com** (Brazil; Mexico; Venezuela, RB; Chile; Argentina; and Spain): www.patagon.com

- **Rava Sociedad de Bolsa** (Argentina): www2.rava.com.ar/cgi-bin/rt/index.cgi

- **Hedging Griffo** (Brazil): www.hedginggriffo.com.br/home/

Annex 4: Smart card providers

Ghana: Mondex e-cash is a multifunctional purse divided into five pockets allowing up to five currencies to be held at a time. It can also be used across open networks such as telephony or the Internet. Mondex Ghana Ltd. controls Ghana s Mondex e-cash franchise. www.mondex.com

Hong Kong, China: i.Life card is a multifunctional card providing credit, debit, and other services. The card is offered by Hongkong and Shanghai Banking Corporation Limited. www.hsbc.com.hk/hk/warning.htm

India: an e-purse is targeted at micropayments and an EMV-compliant debit card is intended for higher-value day-to-day transactions. Sponsors of this program are Proton World (PW) and Alittleworld.com Private Limited (ALW).
www.protonworld.com/press/releases/press63index.htm

Indonesia: the Paspor BCA/Maestro/Cirrus card provides PIN-based online real time debit. The card is offered by MasterCard and BCA.
www.mastercard.com/about/press/pressreleases.cgi?id=3444

Korea, Rep. of: the Mondex e-cash , MasterCard M/Chip» card, and Kookmin Credit Card provides credit, debit, and other services. The card is offered by MasterCard Korea.
www.epaynews.com/archives/index.cgi?ref=browse&f=view&id=982251131212120150500

Korea, Rep. of: A multiapplication card with an electronic purse and credit application is offered by the Pusan Bank of Korea, Rep. of
www.cardtech.faulknergray.com/arch00.htm

Korea, Rep. of: Visa Cash: The Visa Cash card is loaded or has a predefined value, and is designed for secure payments over the Internet and mobile phones, and for low-value purchases.
www.cardtech.faulknergray.com/arch00.htm

Latin America and the Caribbean: The Visa Cash card is loaded or has a predefined value, and is designed for secure payments over the Internet and mobile phones, and for low-value purchases.
www.protonworld.com/press/releases/press47index.htm

Nigeria: The e-purse card relies on Proton technology and is licensed by the Securecard Trust Group.
www.cardtech.faulknergray.com/arch00.htm

Philippines: The Visa Cash card is loaded or has a predefined value, and is designed for secure payments over the Internet and mobile phones, and for low-value purchases. www.cardtech.faulknergray.com/arch00.htm

Singapore: A cash withdrawal card is offered by the Network for Electronic Transfers and local banks.
www.nets.com.sg/news/article.php?artID=11

Singapore: The CashCard‹ TopUp on mobile phones system uses a dual-slot mobile phoe, a smart ATM card, and a HomeNETS PIN. It is offered by the Network for Electronic Transfers and local banks.
www.nets.com.sg/news/article.php?artID=5

South Africa: The Visa Cash card is loaded or has a predefined value, and is designed for secre payments over the Internet and mobile phones, and for low-value purchases. www.cardtech.faulknergray.com/arch00.htm

Thailand: The Visa Cash card is loaded or has a predefined value, and is designed for secure payments over the Internet and mobile phones, and for low-value purchases.
www.businessinthailandmag.com/archive/jul00/29.html

Turkey: Garanti Bank offers a multifunctional card that provides credit, debit, and other services.
www.cardtech.faulknergray.com/arch00.htm

Venezuela, RB: Mondex e-cash is a multifunctional purse divided into five pockets allowing up to five currencies to be held at a time. It can also be used across open networks such as telephony or the Internet. http://www.mondex.com/

Annex 5: E-finance examples

Insurance

China: Sohu.com, a web portal, and Taikang Online, an insurer www.chinaonline.com/industry/financial/NewsArchive/Secure/2001/March/C01030606.asp

Hong Kong, China: Re2R s online open exchange of insurance risk and reinsurance capacities. www.re2re.com/

Mexico: Mexican insurer Grupo Nacional Provincial S.A. will begin offering online Mexican tourist automobile policies through a joint venture with International Insurance Group Inc. www.mexicaninsuranceonline.com

Philippines: Yapster s online insurance service. www.yapster.com/ and www.2insureall.com/

Russian Federation: Renaissance Insurance Group, an e-insurance agency in the Russian Federation. www.renins.com

Various Asian countries: DollarDEX Customized Travel Insurance. www.dollardex.com/insurance/travel/index.cfm?show=travel_moreinfo.cfm

Various Asian countries: Asia s fully online insurance product, from DollarDEX. www.dollardex.com/press/index.cfm?show=i_insurance.htm

Microfinance

Bangladesh: Grameen Bank and Grameen Phone s mobile phone project in rural Bangladesh. www.cisp.org/imp/december_99/12_99camp.htm and www.nation-online.com/200002/17/n0021706.htm#BODY8

Various countries: PlaNet Finance project using the Internet to refinance microfinance institutions. www.planetfinance.org

Various countries: UNCTAD s Virtual Microfinance Market. www.vmm.dpn.ch/

Small and medium-size enterprises

Ghana: Computerized Mobile Bank, an initiative of Advanced Engineering Design and Research Corporation. http://pacific.worldbank.org/ext/results.jsp?DOC_QUERY_TERMS= Computerized+Mobile+Bank%2C+an+initiative+of+Advanced+Engineering+ Design+and+Research+Corporation.&QUERY_TREATMENT=ANY_TERMS &x=39&y=12

Hong Kong, China: SMEloan, a provider of online financing for small and medium-size enterprises.
www.gorillasia.com/tc/readarticle?id=1524

Vietnam: MeetVietnam, an Internet trading tool for small and medium-size enterprises.
www.ifc.org

Various countries: CitiBusiness in the Czech Republic, India, and Hungary
www.citibank.com and www.citibusinessdirect.com

Various countries: The Tradehub Virtual MasterCard.
www.mastercard.com/about/press/pressreleases.cgi?id=321

Various countries: PrideAfrica s virtual information and services network and smart cards for small and medium-size enterprises. www.prideafrica.com/

Various countries: The International Finance Corporation s E-Finance Small Business Initiative.
www.worldbank.org/html/fpd/privatesector/sme.htm and www.ifc.org/sme/

Communications infrastructure

International Telecommunication Union. *www.itu.org*

Public key infrastructure and security

American Society for Industrial Security: The American Society for Industrial Security (ASIS) is the largest international educational organization for security professionals, with over 32,000 members worldwide. ASIS is dedicated to increasing the effectiveness and productivity of security professionals by developing educational programs and materials that focus on both the fundamentals and the most recent advancements in security management. www.asisonline.org

Attrition.org: Documents hacker attacks worldwide.
www.attrition.org

BITS: BITS, the Technology Group for The Financial Services Roundtable, was formed by the CEOs of the largest bank-holding institutions in the United States as the strategic brain trust for the financial services industry in the e-commerce arena. www.bitsinfo.org

CERT: The CERT' Coordination Center (CERT/CC) is a center of Internet security expertise. It is located at the Software Engineering Institute, a federally funded research and development center operated by Carnegie Mellon University. www.cert.org

Hong Kong Monetary Authority: The Authority provides information on the security of banking transactions over the Internet.
www.info.gov.hk/hkma/eng/guide/guide_no/guide_1511xb.htm

Internet Security System: Internet Security Systems (ISS), founded in 1994, is the world s leading provider of security management solutions for the Internet. Headquartered in Atlanta, Georgia, ISS has additional offices throughout the United States, as well as international operations throughout Asia, Australia, Europe, and Latin America. www.iss.net

MSNBC: MSNBC maintains a comprehensive, timely technology section on its Website. http://search.msn.com

National Infrastructure Protection Center: Established in 1998, the NIPC s mission is to serve as the U.S. government s focal point for threat assessment, warning, investigation, and response for threats or attacks against critical infrastructure including telecommunications, ener gy, banking and finance, water systems, government operations, and emergency services. www.nipc.gov

SearchSecurity.com: Provides an aggregation of the information security content on the Internet, as well as original columns and a highly targeted search engine. www.searchsecurity.com

Privacy and information

www.privacy.org

www.astalavista.box.sk

ZDNet: ZDNet s mission is to be a premier full-service destination for people looking to buy, use, and learn more about technology.

www.zdnn.com

www.whitehats.com

References

Abrahams, Shane. 1999. Internet Economy. *Asian Business* (August).

ACCI N Fall Ventures. 1999. Palm Pilots: Lending Efficiency to Microcredit. [www.accion.org/press/main.asp]

Agenor, Pierre-Richard, Joshua Aizenman, and Alexander Hoffmaister. 1999. Contagion, Bank Lending Spreads and Output Fluctuations. Policy Research Working Paper 2186. World Bank, Washington, D.C.

Aggarwal, Reena. 2000. Stabilization Activities by Underwriters after Initial Public Offerings. *Journal of Finance* 55 (3): 1075-1103.

Allen, Franklin, and Anthony Santomero. 1999. What Do Financial Intermediaries Do? University of Philadelphia, Philadelphia, Penn.

Armstrong, Illena. 2001. Managed Service Providers Flex Their Infosecurity Muscles. *SC Magazine*, 12 January.

Baca, Rudy. 2000. The Building Blocks of Growth in the New Economy: A Guide to Global Investment Precursors in Telecom, Internet, and E-Commerce. Legg Mason Precursor Group, New York, N.Y.

Barth, James R., Gerard Caprio, and Ross Levine. 1999. Financial Regulation and Performance: Cross-Country Evidence. Policy Research Working Paper 2037. World Bank, Washington, D.C.

. Forthcoming. Bank Regulation and Supervision: What Works Best? World Bank, Washington, D.C.

Baumol, William J., John C. Panzar, and Robert D. Willig, with contributions by Elizabeth E. Bailey, Dietrich Fischer, and Herman C. Quirmbach. 1982. *Contestable Markets and the Theory of Industry Structure*. New York: Harcourt Brace Jovanovich.

Bell, Simon, Leora Klapper, Annomalai Nagavelli, and Robert Schware. 2001. The Delivery of Financial Services through the Post Office Savings Bank. World Bank, Washington, D.C.

Benston, George J. 2000. Consumer Protection as Justification for Regulating Financial Services Firms and Products. *Journal of Financial Services Research* 17 (3): 277-301.

Berger, Allen N., Rebecca Demsetz, and Philip Strahan. 1998. The Consolidation of the Financial Services Industry: Causes, Consequences and Implications for the Future. Federal Reserve Board, Washington, D.C.

Berger, Allen, Robert deYoung, Hesna Genay, and Gregory Udell. 2000. Globalization of Financial Institutions: Evidence from Cross-Border Banking Performance. Federal Reserve Bank of Chicago. Forthcoming in *Brookings-Wharton Papers in Financial Services,* vol. 3. Washington, D.C.

Bestwire. 2000. Grupo Nacional to Underwrite Online Mexican Tourist Auto Policies Source. Emerging Markets Information Services (May).

Biashara News Letter. 2000. Various articles. 5 (1).

BIS (Bank for International Settlements). 1999. Retail Payments in Selected Countries: A Comparative Study. Basel, Switzerland.

. 2000. International Banking and Financial Market Developments. *Quarterly Review*. Basel, Switzerland.

Blume, Marshall E. 2000. The Structure of the US Equity Markets. University of Pennsylvania, Philadelphia, Penn.

Board of Governors. 1997. Report to the Congress on the Application of the Electronic Fund Transfer Act to Electronic Stored-Value Products. Federal Reserve System, Washington, D.C.

Bond Market Association. 2000a. Bond Leaders Forecast Economic Conditions and Business Trends. *Bond Market Association Research* (February).

——. 2000b. Bond Market: News from the Bond Market Association. *Bond Market Association Research* (August/September and October).

——. 2000c. E-Commerce in the Fixed-Income Markets. *Bond Market Association 2000 Review of Electronic Transaction Systems.*

Bossone, Biagio, and Larry Promisel. 1999. The Role of Financial Self-regulation in Developing Economies. Website Policy Note. World Bank, Washington, D.C. [http://wbwebapps2.worldbank.org/wwwfinance/html/self-regulation-in-developing-.html]

Calomiris, Charles, and Robert Litan. 1999. Financial Regulation in a Global Marketplace. Brookings Institution, Washington, D.C.

Calvo, Guillermo, and Enrique Mendoza. 1998. Rational Herd Behavior and the Globalization of Securities Markets. University of Maryland, College Park, Md.

Chauvel, Bernard, and Lawrence Uhlick. 1999. Global Survey 1999: Regulatory and Market Developments. Institute of International Bankers, New York, N.Y.

Chaves, Rodrigo, Susana Sanchez, Saul Schor, and Emil Tesliuc. 2001. Financial Markets, Credit Constraints, and Investment in Rural Romania. Enviromentally and Socially Sustainable Development Technical Paper. World Bank, Washington, D.C.

Claessens, Stijn, and Marion Jansen, eds. 2000. *The Internationalization of Financial Services.* Boston, Mass.: Kluwer Academic Press for the World Bank and World Trade Organization.

Claessens, Stijn, and Daniela Klingebiel. 1999. Alternative Frameworks for Providing Financial Services. Policy Research Working Paper 2189. World Bank, Washington, D.C.

Claessens, Stijn, Thomas Glaessner, and Daniela Klingebiel. 2001. E-finance in Emerging Markets: Is Leapfrogging Possible? Financial Sector Discussion Paper 7. World Bank, Washington, D.C.

——. 2000. Electronic Finance: Reshaping the Financial Landscape around the World. Financial Sector Discussion Paper 4. World Bank, Washington, D.C.

Claessens, Stijn, Daniela Klingebiel, and Sergio Schmukler. Forthcoming. The Future of Stock Markets in Emerging Economies. Brookings-Wharton Paper on Financial Services.

Clarke, George, Robert Cull, Laura D Amato, and Andrea Molinari. 1999. The Effect of Foreign Entry on Argentina s Domestic Banking Sector. Policy Research Working Paper 2158. World Bank, Washington, D.C.

Copenhagen Stock Exchange. 2001. The Electra Trading Systems. Copenhagen Stock Exchange. [www.xcse.dk/uk/marked/]

Corrigan, E. Gerard. 2000. Are Banks Special: A Revisitation. *The Region* (special issue). Federal Reserve Bank of Minneapolis. [http://woodrow.mpls.frb.fed.us/pubs/region/00-03/corrigan.html]

Credit Suisse First Boston Global Bank Team. 1999. Special Internet Banking Review. New York.

Crockett, Andrew, and William McDonough. 1998. Managing Change in Payments Systems. BIS Policy Paper 4. Bank for International Settlements, Monetary and Economic Department, Basel, Switzerland.

Crumley, Bruce. 2000. A Plastic Brain in Your Pocket. *Time*, 16 October.

Demsetz, Rebecca, Marc Saidenberg, and Philip Strahan. 1996. Banks with Something to Lose: The Disciplinary Role of Franchise Value. *Economic Policy Review*. Federal Reserve Bank of New York.

Depository Trust and Clearing Corporation. 2000. A White Paper to the Industry on the Future of CCPs. Washington, D.C.

Dewatripont, Mathias, and Jean Tirole, 1994. *The Prudential Regulation of Banks*. Cambridge, Mass.: MIT Press.

Diamond, Douglas, and Philip H. Dybvig. 1983. Bank Runs, Deposit Insurance and Liquidity. *Journal of Political Economy* 91 (June): 401—19.

Diamond, Douglas, and Raghuram Rajan. 1998. Liquidity Risk, Liquidity Creation and Financial Fragility: A Theory of Banking. Working Paper 476. University of Chicago, Center for Research in Security Prices, Chicago, Ill.

——. 1999. A Theory of Bank Capital. University of Chicago, Chicago, Ill.

Diwan, Parag, and Shammi Kapoor. 2000. Bharat s Cyber and E-Commerce Laws with Information Technology Act. Bharat Publishing House, India.

The Economist. 2000a. The Internet and the Law. 13 January.

——. 2000b. A Survey of E-Management. 2 October.

——. 2000c. A Survey of the New Economy. 6 November.

——. 2001. A Survey of Global Equity Markets. 5 May.

Edwards, Franklin. 1999. Hedge Funds and the Collapse of Long-Term Capital Management. *Journal Of Economic Perspectives* 13 (spring): 189—210.

Egland, Kori L., Karen Furst, Daniel E. Nolle, and Douglas Robertson. 1998. Banking over the Internet. *Quarterly Journal* 17 (4): 25-30.

Emmons, William. 1997. Recent Developments in Wholesale Payments Systems. *Review* (November/December). Federal Reserve Bank of St. Louis, St. Louis, Miss.

Enterprise for Development International. 2000. Ford Foundation Study on Development Funding for Poverty Alleviation (DFPA). Country Briefing Document: Nigeria. Washington, D.C.

Enz, Rudolf. 2000. The S-Curve Relation between Per-Capita Income and Insurance Penetration. *Geneva Papers on Risk and Insurance* 3 (25): 396-406.

Euromoney. 2000a. New Credit Risk Portal Announced. December.

——. 2000b. World Bank Readies Online Trading. December.

European Central Bank. 1999a. The Effects of Technology on the EU Banking Systems. Frankfurt, Germany.

——. 1999b. Possible Effects of EMU on the EU Banking Systems in the Medium to Long Term. Frankfurt, Germany.

Fargo, Jason. 2001. Bank Cards Heed the Smart Card Call. *Credit Card Management* (January).

Financial Stability Forum. 2000. Executive Summary. Basel, Switzerland.

Financial Times. 2001. Special Report on Information Technology. February.

Freixas, Xavier, and Jean-Charles Rochet. 1998. *Microeconomics of Banking*. Cambridge, Mass.: MIT Press.

Furfine, Craig. 2000. Empirical Evidence on the Need for a Lender of Last Resort. Bank for International Settlements, Basel, Switzerland.

Furst, Karen, William W. Lang, and Daniel E. Nolle. 1998. Technological Innovation in Banking and Payments: Industry Trends and Implications for Banks. *Quarterly Journal* 17 (3): 23-31.

——. 2000. Internet Banking: Developments and Prospects.   Working Paper 2000-9. Comptroller of the Currency Administrator of National Banks, Washington, D.C.

Furst, Karen, Thomas Glaessner, and Thomas Kellermann. 2001. Internet Security and Financial Services. World Bank, Washington, D.C.

Garrigues, Charlie. 2000. Estonia Supervision Mission. World Bank, Washington, D.C.

Gilbert, R. Alton. 1998. Did the Fed s Founding Improve the Efficiency of the U.S. Payments System? *Review* (May/June). Federal Reserve Bank of St. Louis, St. Louis, Miss.

Glaessner, Thomas. 1993. External Regulation Vs. Self-Regulation: What Is the Right Mix? The Perspective of the Emerging Securities Markets of Latin America and the Caribbean. Regional Studies Program Report. World Bank, Latin America and Caribbean Technical Department, Washington, D.C.

Glaessner, Thomas, Jeppe Ladekarl, and Leora Klapper. 2000. India: Financial Sector Strategy Paper. World Bank, Washington, D.C.

Goldberg, Linda, Gerard Dages, and Daniel Kinney. 1999. Lending in Emerging Markets: Foreign and Domestic Banks Compared. Federal Reserve Bank of New York, New York, N.Y.

Goldstein, Andrea, and David O Connor. E-Commerce for Development: Prospects and Policy Issues. Organisation for Economic Co-operation and Development, Development Centre, Paris.

Goodwin, Procter, and Hoar LLP. 2000. Central Bank of Jordan E-Commerce Legislation. Harvard University, Cambridge, Mass.

Green, Edward J. 1999. Money and Debt in the Structure of Payments. *Federal Reserve Bank of Minneapolis Quarterly Review* (spring): 13-29.

Gual, Jordi. 1999. Deregulation, Integration, and Market Structure in European Banking. *Journal of the Japanese and International Economies* 13: 372—96.

Guttentag, Jack. 2000. Multi-Lender Mortgage Websites. International Union for Housing Finance, Chicago, Ill.

Hilton, Andrew. 2000. Internet Banking: A Fragile Flower. Where s the Killer App ? Centre for the Study of Financial Innovation, London.

Hitachi Research Institute. 2000. Electronic Money. [http://semiconductor.hitachi.com/smartcard/em/]

Hodes, Michael, Gregory Hall, and Lawrence Rosenberg. 1999. Issues and Outlook 2000: United States; eFinance. Goldman Sachs and Co., Investment Research, New York, N.Y.

Housing and Commercial Bank. 2000. Becoming a World Class Retail Bank: 1999 Operating Results and 2000 Plan. Seoul, Republic of Korea.

Hughes, Joseph P., William Lang, Loretta Mester, and Choon-Geol Moon. 1998. The Dollars and Sense of Bank Consolidation. Working Paper 98-10. Federal Reserve Bank of Philadelphia, Research Department, Philadelphia, Penn.

Hussey, Chris, Maria Gonzalez, Michael Parekh, Vik Mehta, and Luanne Zurlo. 2000. Latin American Internet Primer. Goldman Sachs and Co., Investment Research, New York, N.Y.

ICICI. 2001. ICICI: India s Leader in E-finance. Mumbai, India. [www.icici.com]

Institute of Institutional Bankers. 1999. *Global Survey: Regulatory and Market Developments.* New York.

International Telecommunication Union. 1999. *World Telecommunication Development Report 1999.* Geneva.

International Union for Housing Finance. 2000. How Do You Measure Success in Housing Finance? Chicago, Ill.

Intven, Hank, Jeremy Oliver, and Edgardo Sepulveda. 2000. *Telecomunications Regulation Handbook.* Washington, D.C.: World Bank.

IOSCO (International Organization of Securities Commissions). 1998. Internet Task Force. Madrid, Spain. [www.iosco.org]

Isimbabi, Michael. 1994. The Stock Market Perception of Industry Risk and the Separation of Banking and Commerce. *Journal of Banking & Finance* 18.

Issing, Otmar. 2000. The Globalization of Financial Markets. European Central Bank, Frankfurt, Germany .

James, John. 1998. Commentary. *Review* (May/June). Federal Reserve Bank of St. Louis, St. Louis, Mo.

Kahn, Alfred Edward. 1998. *The Economics of Regulation: Principles and Institutions.* Cambridge, Mass.: MIT Press.

Kashyap, Anil K., Raghuram Rajan, and Jeremy Stein. 1999. Banks As Liquidity Providers: An Explanation for the Co-Existence of Lending and Deposit-Taking. University of Chicago, Chicago, Ill.

Kelly, Dean. 1998. How an Insurance Industry Global Extranet Failed to Achieve Critical Mass Despite Market Readiness and Stake Holder Dominance: A Case Study of the World Insurance Network Initiative. New Jersey Institute of Technology, School of Management, Newark, N.J.

Key, Sydney. Forthcoming. GATS 2000: Issues for the Financial Services Negotiations. Sectoral Studies on Trade in Services. American Enterprise Institute, Washington, D.C.

Khan, Salman, Roy Ramos, and Adrian Tan. 2000. Citibank: An Asian Internet Mandarin in the Making? In *eFinance in Asia, Part 2.* New York: Goldman Sachs and Co., Global Equity Research.

Kim, Jungshik, and Shang-Jin Wei. 1997. The Big Players in the Foreign Exchange Market: Do they Trade on Information or Noise? NBER Working Paper 6256. National Bureau for Economic Research, Cambridge, Mass.

Knox, Robert. 2000. Online Bond Trading Today. Paper presented at the Bond Market Association s Government Operations Conference, 5 October, Couer d Alene, Idaho.

KPMG. 2000. Frontiers in Finance: If E-Business Is Business, Then Strategy Is E-Strategy. Washington, D.C.

Krishnamurthi, Sudhir. 2000. The Future of Global Investments. World Bank, Washington, D.C.

Lacker, Jeffrey, Jeffrey Walker, and John Weinberg. 1999. The Fed s Entry into Check Clearing Reconsidered. *Economic Quarterly.* Federal Reserve Bank of Richmond, Richmond, Va.

La Porta, Ricardo, Fernando Lopez-de-Silanes, and Andrei Shleifer. 2000. Government Ownership of Banks. Harvard University, Cambridge, Mass.

Maggiotto, Rocco. 2000. Defining Tomorrow s Leading Financial Services Institution. Pricewaterhouse Coopers, Global Financial Services Leadership Team, New York, N.Y.

Maheshwari, Vijai. 2000. Baltic Finance and Investment: IT Pioneers Create Frenzy of Activity. *Financial Times Survey*, 19 May.

McAndrews, James. 1997. Banking and Payment System Stability in an Electronic Money World. Working Paper 97-9. Federal Reserve Bank of Philadelphia, Philadelphia, Penn.

McAndrews, James, and William Roberts. 2000. Payment Intermediation and the Origins of Banking. *Journal of Economic Literature Classification.*

McKinsey, Kitty. 2001. In the Cards. *Far Eastern Economic Review.* 12 January.

Merton, Robert C. 1995. A Functional Perspective of Financial Intermediation. *Journal of the Financial Management Association* 24 (2).

Miehlbradt, A., and T. Chua. 1999. Information and Communications Services for Micro and Small Enterprises in the Philippines: A Synthesis Paper. Microenterprise Best Practices Project, Development Alternatives/USAID, Bethesda, Md.

Mishkin, Frederic, and Philip Strahan. 1999. What Will Technology Do to Financial Structure? In Robert E. Litan and Anthony Santomero, eds., *Brookings-Wharton Papers on Financial Services.* Washington, D.C.: Brookings Institution.

Mobile Commerce World Magazine. 2001. Dial M for Banking. January .

Mondex. 1999. 17 Central Banks Make Mondex E-Cash Standard in Africa. [http://mondex.com]

———. 2000. Mondex Ghana Ltd. Selects Hitachi Europe Ltd. for Its $2M Mondex Electronic Cash Solution. [http://mondex.com]

Morawski, Edward. 2001. Net Currency . *Red Herring* (January): 84-85.

OECD (Organisation for Economic Co-operation and Development). 2000. Guidelines for Consumer Protection in the Context of Electronic Commerce. Paris.

———. 2001. International and Regional Bodies: Activities and Initiatives in Electronic Commerce. Paris.

Osterberg, William, and James Thomson. 1998. Bank Notes and Stored-Value Cards: Stepping Lightly into the Past. Economic Commentary. Federal Reserve Bank of Cleveland, Research Department, Cleveland, Ohio.

———. 1999. Banking Consolidation and Correspondent Banking. Federal Reserve Bank of Cleveland, Research Department, Cleveland, Ohio.

Padhi, Michael. 2000. Banks Selling Insurance: Tricky Business? Federal Reserve Bank of Atlanta, Atlanta, Ga. [http://www.frbatlanta.org/publica/finan_update/v12n4/fu_v12n4_1.html]

Paulson, Joanne. 1998. Financial Services for the Urban Poor . Policy Research Working Paper 2016. World Bank, Washington, D.C.

PC Magazine. 2001. Know Who I Am. 16 January . [www.pcmag.com]

Prague Stock Exchange. 2001. Trading System. [http://www.pse.cz/default.asp?language=English]

Radecki, Lawrence, 1999. Banks Payments-Driven Revenues. *Economic Policy Review.* Federal Reserve Bank of New York, New York, N.Y.

Ramos, Roy, Daniel Abut, David Townsend, Paul Formanko, Salman Khan, Chunsoo Lim, W. Matanachai, Sherry Chung, Carol Cheung, and Adrian Tan. 1999. Will the Internet Shake Up Asia s Banks? In *eFinance in Asia, Part 1*. New York: Goldman Sachs and Co., Asia Financial Services, Investment Research.

R ller , Lars-Hendrik, and Leonard Waverman. 2000. Telecommunications Infrastructure and Economic Development: A Simultaneous Approach. Working Paper 2399. Centre for Economic Policy Research, Washington, D.C.

Sachs, Jeffrey D. 2000. Readiness for the Networked World: A Guide for Developing Countries. Harvard University, Center for International Development, Cambridge, Mass.

Saidenberg, Marc, and Philip Strahan. 1999. Are Banks Still Important for Financing Large Businesses? *Current Issues in Economics and Finance*. Federal Reserve Bank of New York, Research and Market Analysis Group, New York, N.Y.

Salomon Smith Barney. 1999. *The Salomon Smith Barney Guide to World Equity Markets*. London.

Sands, Peter. 2000. 7 th European Banking Report Advisory Board Meeting. McKinsey & Co, London.

Shafer, Scott T. 2001. Trading on Innovation. *Red Herring* (January): 76-81.

Shapiro, Carl, and Hal R. Varian, 1999. *Information Rules: A Strategic Guide to the Network Economy*. Boston, Mass.: Harvard Business School Press.

Simons, Katerina, and Joanna Stavins. 1998. Has Antitrust Policy in Banking Become Obsolete? *New England Economic Review* (March/April). Federal Reserve Bank of Boston, Boston, Mass.

Sirtaine, Sophie. 2001. On the Services Offered by Post Offices in Various Countries. World Bank, Finance and Private Sector Development, Washington, D.C.

Solomon, Elinor Harris. 1999. What Should Regulators Do about Consolidation and Electronic Money? *Journal of Banking & Finance* 23: 645—53.

Sood, Rakesh, Richard Strauss, Michael Hodes, Robert Hottensen, Thomas Cholnoky, Joan Zief, Elizabeth Werner, J.D. Miller, and Jonathan Tukman. 1999. E-Commerce Financial Services at a Glance: United States. Goldman Sachs and Co., Investment Research, New York, N.Y.

Stavins, Joanna. 1999. Checking Accounts: What Do Banks Offer and What Do Consumers Value? *New England Economic Review* (March/April). Federal Reserve Bank of Boston, Boston, Mass.

Steering Committee on the Enhancement of the Financial Infrastructure in Hong Kong. 1999. An E-frastructure for a Leading E-economy. Hong Kong.

Stein, Tom. 2001. Cash Servers. *Red Herring* (January): 86.

Summers, Bruce, and Akinari Horii. 1994. Large-Value Transfer Systems. In Bruce Summers, ed., *The Payments System: Design, Management, and Supervision*. Washington, D.C.: International Monetary Fund.

Sveriges RiksBank. 2000. *Yearbook*. Stockholm.

Ungwu, Enitar. 2000. Gemcard Tackles Rural Banking. *Lagos Post Express*. [http://allafrica.com/stories/200011270441.html]

University of Texas. 2000. The Internet and the Future of Financial Markets: Combining Technology with Established Financial Market Mechanisms. University of Texas, Center for Research in Electronic Commerce, Austin.

U.S. Securities and Exchange Commission. 2000. Federal Regulation of Securities Activity on the Internet. Division of Market Regulation, Washington, D.C.

Wallman, Steven. 1999. The Information Technology Revolution and Its Impact on Regulation and Regulatory Structure. In Robert E. Litan and Anthony Santomero, eds., *Brookings-Wharton Papers on Financial Services*. Washington, D.C.: Brookings Institution.

Weinberg, John. 1997. The Organization of Private Payment Networks. *Economic Quarterly Volume* 83 (2). Federal Reserve Bank of Richmond, Richmond, Va.

Werthamer, N. Richard, and Susan Raymond. 1997. Technology and Finance: The Electronic Markets. In *Technological Forecasting and Social Change: An International Journal*. New York: Elsevier Science.

Wisekey. 2000. Global E-Security. Geneva.

World Bank. 1999. *World Development Report 1998/99: Knowledge for Development*. New York: Oxford University Press.

. 2000a. E-Finance Brief: Legal Developments Related to E-Finance. Washington, D.C.

. 2000b. *Global Development Finance*. Washington, D.C.

. 2000c. Improving Taxpayer Service and Facilitating Compliance in Singapore. PREMnote 48. Washington, D.C.

. 2000d. *World Development Indicators 2000*. Washington, D.C.

. 2001. *Finance for Growth: Policy Choices in a Volatile World*. Policy Research Report. New York: Oxford University Press.

Zeichick, Alan. 2001. Smart Cards Explained. *Red Herring* (January): 82-83.

Bibliographical Note

Box 1: Mobile phones: The developing world s technological springboard. Information was garnered from the International Telecommunication Union s *World Telecommunication Development Report 1999.* A. Romero describes these technological advances in his article Cell Phone Sur ge among the World s Poor in the 12 December 2000 *New York Times* (www.nyt.com).

Box 4: Leapfrogging around the globe: Estonia, Republic of Korea, and Brazil. Estonia s progress in information technology is discussed in Maheshwari (2000). Charlie Garrigues s (2000) back to office report on the Estonia Payment System Project provided valuable information. The data on the number of online clients are from the Baltic News Service (2000) . The International Telecommunication Union s World Telecommunication Indicators Database (1999) also provided information (www.itu.org).

Box 14: Insurance: E-financeable? The use of the Internet in the insurance industry is discussed in Kelly (1998). For further information on the Renaissance Insurance Group, see the company s Website (www.renins.com). The information on online automobile policies in Mexico is from Bestwire (2000). The examples on Yapster, Re2Re, DollarDEX, and China are from their Websites (www.yapster.com, www.re2re.com, www.dollardex.com, www.chinaonline.com).

Box 15: E-finance for small and medium-size enterprises. The SMEloan example draws largely on the information provided on SMEloan s Website (www.smeloan.com) and Gorillasia.com (www.gorillasia.com/tc/readarticle?id=1524). The examples on DrumNet and Sunlink are from *Biashara News Letter* (2000), Pride Africa s Website (www.prideafrica.com), and www.geocities.com/Starsys2000/page3.html. The information on CitiBusiness Direct comes mainly from the Citibank and Citibusiness Direct Websites (www.citibank.com and www.citibusinessdirect.com).

Box 16: Microfinance and e-finance a viable match? The factors that hinder the use of information technology in microfinance institutions are discussed in Miehlbradt and Chua (1999). The E Bank example in South Africa is from Paulson (1998), the Gemcard example in Nigeria is from Ungwu (2000), the ACCI N Palm Pilot example is from ACCI N Fall Ventures (1999), and the PlaNet Finance and Virtual Microfinance Market information is from their Websites (www.planetfinance.org/en/institutionnel/index.htm and www.vmm.dpn.ch/).